For Elsbeth

ISBN 978-0-9565063-4-4

Printed and Bound in Ireland

Illustrations by Dympna Driscoll

Victorian Images Courtesy of Thomas Etty Seeds Esq.

Editing by Anna-Maya Pawlowski

Printed on Recycled Paper

The Self-Sufficient Garden

Klaus Laitenberger

Contents

Introduction

I grew up in a small village in South Germany next to the beautiful Neckar River winding its way along steep vineyards. The water was so polluted that we were not allowed to even touch it. Then the neighbouring Black Forest started to die.

In April 1986, the Chernobyl disaster happened and the nuclear cloud came directly over us. Life and business continued as usual for most people.

Nothing was the same for me after that. I knew that a lot of things needed to change. Many things did change – the Neckar River is a lot cleaner now, there are fish again and some of the forests are recovering.

I'm writing this because I can see the same problems appearing here in this beautiful island of Ireland. Our rivers and lakes are polluted with numerous chemicals (weed killers and fertilisers).

These chemicals have even found their way into the groundwater and are polluting wells. To have polluted water in a country with such a low population and so little industry is beyond comprehension. The solution would be so simple and effective and we could swim and drink water from every lake and river in Ireland.

I know I am too extreme – I would ban the use of harmful chemicals that are polluting our environment.

I can sense a major shift coming. I'm rejuvenated by a strange positivity and I can feel that change is coming soon. So many people now realise that we have to live in harmony with nature – that we are a part of nature. We can no longer view nature simply as a means for providing resources for our industries.

What scares me though is how we have become so separated from nature. Half of the people in the world now live in cities, most people couldn't identify trees or wildflowers, children get less outdoor activity than what is given to prisoners for mental health - phones, gadgets, games – everything has become so fast.

This was one of the few good side effects of Covid-19 – the pause button was pressed. It was as if nature, or Mother Earth, asked us to sit back and reflect. I'm sure millions of people have rediscovered the little miracles of nature during this time and will find it difficult to get back into the 'fast' world.

A good start is to grow some of our own food, to connect with nature in the garden and then get a glimpse of the real world that surrounds us - the miracle of a seed germinating or a potato sprout emerging from the soil. Digging a basket of potatoes, cooking them and eating a delicious meal with your family – it is so simple – you work for it and it will nourish you infinitely more. As well as that, you possibly leave this plot of land in a better state than when you started.

There are more and more people who are growing their own food again and even starting small market gardens. I recently asked a young organic market gardener why she chose this profession as there are far easier ways of making a living. Her answer was, "Because it's cool." This is a great shift in mindset and hopefully reflects a much wider population.

Up to quite recently, food growing was considered old-fashioned and too much like hard work. It's easier to buy food from a shop. Now it's cool to grow your own food and you'll get the extra benefit of good physical exercise and fresh air. Times are changing.

When you ask people to guess how much land you would need to feed a family with vegetables for most of the year the answer is often an acre or two.
This is completely wrong. In this book, I'll outline three vegetable cropping plans ranging from 50m² to 400m². A plot of about 200m² (partial self-sufficiency) to 400m² (full self-sufficiency) would be enough to feed a family of two adults and two children.
And 400m² is 1/10 of an acre (an acre is about 4,000m²). It is fantastic news that one acre can feed 10 families or 25 families per hectare (one hectare is 10,000m²).

Scope of the book

In this book, I only cover the 30 most important vegetable crops. Many minor or fiddly crops have been omitted only because it would make the book and the planning too complex. You can easily fit them into your crop plan. In a garden there is always some extra space.

One important thing to realise is that not all crops will be perfect, there will also be some complete failures of certain crops and this happens to the best of growers.

The crop plans are based on a family of 2 adults and 2 children that consume a lot of vegetables. The first crop plan is for a small garden and specialises only on high-value and value for space crops, the second crop plan is for easy-to-grow staple crops that will fill your store. The third crop plan is for the completely self-sufficient garden with 300m² outdoor garden and 90m² of a polytunnel. If all crops are performing well there will be a lot vegetables to give away and new friends to be made.

How much time is needed?

The first two gardens can be done with very little time commitments – a few days to get it all started in spring and then just a couple hours in the evening or half a day at the weekend.

The completely self-sufficient garden, however, requires a more concerted family effort. If you do not have a garden yet, it will take time (or good machinery) to get the ground ready and the beds formed. After that it will take two people for one full day at the weekend and half an hour some evenings to maintain the garden.

Throughout the book, I'm quite precise with figures and sowing dates because I think this is helpful for people to get started, but these are not written in stone. Try them out, modify the techniques and sowing dates as it suits you. The beauty of gardening is that there are many right ways of doing things. No two gardeners will ever be the same. After reading a number of books from different authors, visiting gardens and trying it all out yourself you will be in danger of getting confused with so much conflicting information thrown at you from all sides. Don't worry, simply pick out the best tips and create your own method that suits you and your garden.

I couldn't write a book on self-sufficient gardening without mentioning the hero and pioneer of self-sufficiency, John Seymour.

I was lucky to have met him once when he came to Leitrim and stayed with us for the weekend while giving a weekend course at the Organic Centre. I'll never forget the philosophical discussions and pints in the local pub. One thing I clearly remember though was his advice – "Always and wherever you are – you need to be part of the whole community – people and the world around you." He said it far more eloquently than that.

"A preoccupation of the self-sufficient person should be the correct attitude to the land. If it ever comes to pass that we have used up all, or most of, the oil on this planet, we will have to reconsider our attitude to our only real and abiding asset – the land itself. We will one day have to derive our sustenance from what the land, unaided by oil-derived chemicals can produce."

John Seymour

Soil

The most urgent crisis humanity faces is the destruction of our soils – even more urgent than the climate crisis. The United Nations Food and Agriculture Association (FAO) tell us that, globally, we have only 60 harvests left if we continue to destroy our soils. And we do continue! Every minute we lose soil from an area the size of a football pitch and 25 to 30% of the world's agricultural land area has already been degraded.

In most places farming has turned into agri-business. It has become industrial farming with high inputs of chemicals, fertilisers and animal feed, and has led to specialisation of a monocrop or one species of animal on one farm. The traditional mixed farms are disappearing fast.

A mixed farm with various live-stock and crops requires very few inputs.

Therefore, it is resilient to changes in the economy and also more resilient to changing climate conditions.

A typical modern farm buys in animal feed from genetically modified and roundup resistant soy beans from Argentina, genetically modified maize from the US, potassium fertiliser from Canada, phosphorus fertiliser from Morocco and nitrogen fertiliser which is produced through the Haber-Bosch process which requires 5% of the annual world gas consumption. I could go on about pesticides and weed killers.

None of this makes any sense – we can grow food and rear animals without any of these inputs and, as many pioneers in the organic/regenerative movement have shown, with much higher profit margins.

If we learn more about how we can use and benefit from natural ecosystems and cycles, such as natural nitrogen fixation with leguminous plants, and harness mycorrhizal fungi, the easier and more sustainable our gardens and farms will be.

Two side-effects of the industrial, chemical farming method are the degradation of our soils and the pollution of our own natural environment.

If we really want to make a change in the world, we need to make a seismic change to regenerative organic farming and vegetable production. Ireland currently (2020) has 2.4% of its land area certified organic. The EU set a target that each country should achieve 25% of organically farmed land by 2030 – this is a massive step for a better future. Let's just hope that our Department of Agriculture and agricultural colleges are in line with this.

This shift will probably be driven by consumers who are becoming a lot more aware of how food is produced and may choose to eat food that is produced at a local organic market garden or farm.

I have met so many young people who are setting up organic market gardens throughout the country. It's the beginning of a movement for positive change. The one thing they all have in common is the care and love for our Earth and, ultimately, the care of our soil on which all life on Earth depends upon.

If we continue to destroy our soil we are sweeping the carpet away from under our feet.

We need to learn to understand, appreciate, and even start to love our soil and see it as "Mother Earth." Surprisingly soils can regenerate very quickly, even after a couple of years of good husbandry life comes back and proliferates. We need to feed the soil again and the soil will feed the plants and ourselves.

Soil fertility

Everyone dreams about a fertile, free-draining soil, slightly acidic (pH 6-6.8), with a good crumbly structure, rich in nutrients, a high humus content and plenty of soil life. Some may inherit such a garden from our ancestors.

Old walled gardens always have such wonderful soils (unless the soil was removed), but there was also a garden on every old cottage or dwelling. All you need to do is to find it. I would go round with a digging fork and push it into the ground in various places, and wherever it slides in like butter, compared to the hard and more compacted adjacent ground you have struck gold – black gold.

Dig a test hole and see if the soil is darker in colour, more crumbly, check how deep the soil is and look for earthworm channels. This garden could have been abandoned 40 years ago, but the inherent soil fertility is still there.

I have experienced this in a couple of walled gardens which were abandoned a long time ago (over 50 years) but the soil was still the best I've seen and both the crops and soil results confirmed it.

However, not everyone is lucky enough to start off with this precious gift from the past and often we need to improve a poorer soil, but not to worry, this is easy and just as satisfying.

How to improve your soil?

Here are a few tips:

Use of good farmyard manure and/or compost

If we take crops out of the garden we need to give something back again. As a rule of thumb, if I harvest one wheelbarrow of vegetables, I plan to return one wheelbarrow of compost.

Alternatively, spread one wheelbarrow of compost (or composted manure) per 3m² on poor soils or for heavy feeders (e.g. brassicas). On good soil or light feeders (eg. carrots), spread one wheelbarrow of well-decomposed compost per 5m².

It's a good idea to get a load of either horse or cattle manure and mix it into your compost – a few buckets full every week.

Use of mulches

It's the method of covering bare soil with an organic material, such as leaf mould, composted wood chips, lawn mowings, straw, etc. The advantages of mulching are manifold. Mulching prevents weeds, keeps the soil moist, provides food for microorganisms and worms and improves the structure of a soil.

If you could buy screened green waste compost, this would be an excellent mulch, and compared to other mulches you won't need to worry about slugs and snails.

Use of seaweed

A winter mulch of seaweed is highly beneficial to soils. Don't worry about the salt, it will dissolve before you plant your crops the following spring. In a garden close to the sea I cover all the beds in October with a seaweed mulch about 20cm deep. In March, the seaweed has nearly decomposed with only a few tough bits left. It's best to remove the seaweed then and compost it or mulch fruit trees.

Crop rotation

A well-designed rotation can help improve your garden soil. If you include members of the legume family such as peas and beans – they will fix atmospheric nitrogen and deposit it in your soil. You should aim to alternate heavy feeders (or greedy vegetables) with light feeders so you don't exhaust your soil.

Crop diversity

Grow a mixture of different, but compatible, crops in the same bed. There is evidence that increased crop diversity improves soil health, crop production and resilience in changing and abnormal climate and soil conditions.

Green manuring

If you find that your garden has become exhausted, an excellent way for regenerating it is to take out one quarter of your plot and grow a red clover green manure on it every one in four years for a whole year.

Green manures can improve the soil fertility in various ways, either by adding atmospheric nitrogen (legumes), by increasing the organic matter content, by stimulating soil life, by preventing nutrients from leaching, and by growing into lower compacted layers, thus increasing the rooting depth for plants and bringing already lost nutrients back up again.

To dig or not to dig?

This seems quite a controversial argument amongst gardeners. A no-dig system is better for conservation of carbon or organic matter in the soil. As a result, I dig less and less, but there are still times when I feel I need to dig. For example, when I need to convert grassland into a vegetable garden and don't have sufficient compost for mulching or sufficient time to cover the ground for a year to kill off the grass. I would also dig if the ground has become too weedy.

Generally, I simply bio-fork – this means pushing a digging fork into the ground and levering it back 45 degrees and repeating it all along the bed. This loosens the soil without turning it upside down. For a larger garden there are specialist tools available called either 'broad fork' or 'bio fork'.

In countries with wet winters never dig a garden in autumn as most nutrients will be leached out and you'll end up with a swamp. However, you can dig in autumn if you cover the soil with black plastic after digging.

Warning:
In the last few years a number of gardeners sent me photos of distorted vegetables planted in beds that were given composted manures. The plants looked like they were sprayed with a weed killer. Farmers were using a strong weed killer to control docks and thistles which contains Aminopyralid. This chemical goes through the animal's digestive system, through the composting process and even three years later it can still kill your potatoes, tomatoes, beans, peas and a number of other crops.
So before getting manure, ask the farmer if he/she sprayed docks and thistles.
I think it is scary that a harmful chemical that can persist for so long and nothing seems to break it down is permitted for use by farmers and gardeners.

Ground Preparation

Preparing the ground

Getting started

After you have decided on the size and location of your vegetable plot, you can mark it out. Place canes or fence posts at the corners and stand back to look at it and see how it fits into your garden.

Bed preparation - Options

There are various options for getting your soil ready, ranging from very lazy to really hard work. The use of a rotavator to get your ground ready from grass is not advisable as it churns up the soil while still leaving most of the shredded grass sods on the surface ready to regrow within a few days. You'll also form a solid, impenetrable pan where the blades of the rotavator seal the soil beneath.

Option 1: Covering with black plastic for 12 months

This is by far the laziest, but a very effective method for converting your lawn into a productive vegetable plot. In early spring mow your lawn or strim your meadow and then spread a generous amount of cow or horse manure over the grass (about 1 wheelbarrow for every 3 to 4m²).

After that, you cover the whole area with strong black plastic (silage plastic) and secure it well so that the wind won't blow it off. I cover the plastic with a thin layer of semi-decomposed wood-chips. This holds the plastic down securely and is more pleasing to the eye. I also tuck in the edges with a spade.

Sometimes you can get a second-hand piece of plastic from a farmer.

If you wish, you can make small holes (or better a T-Slit) in the plastic roughly every two metres and plant a trailing squash or pumpkin into it. The growth of these will cover the entire area. You'll still get your vegetable plot ready for the following year but also get a great yield of squashes and pumpkins in the first year.

In the following spring (February/March) lift the plastic, collect the slugs which are stuck to it and you'll be amazed by how beautiful the soil is underneath. The only drawback is waiting for 12 months but you can start small in the first year and at the same time prepare a new section for the following year. Then, mark out the beds and path with sticks.

The path should be around 40-50cm wide and the beds around 1-1.3m wide.

You will find that the worms have already done most of the digging and mixing for you during the last 12 months. All you need to do is ruffle up the soil on the beds with a fork and then shovel some of the soil from the paths onto the beds. Let the soil settle for a week (or longer) and then you are ready.

Finally, you finish by levelling and smoothing the surface of the soil with a rake to make a fine-textured seed bed.

Example of covering with black plastic

Option 2: Single digging

Single digging is a lot harder than just covering, but it is great exercise. Never dig if the ground is waterlogged or sticks to your boots otherwise you may cause unnecessary soil compaction. You can dig in late autumn but then you should cover the plot with black plastic to prevent the nutrients from washing out, or you could wait until February/March.

Mark out the plot with a line and take out a trench 40cm wide and about 20cm deep. The soil from this trench should be piled just outside the far side of your plot.

It would be beneficial to loosen the soil at the bottom of the trench with a fork and then add compost or manure to it. Then, start the second row about 15cm wide and invert the soil into the first trench and repeat the loosening of the subsoil with a fork and compost application. Then, you continue with rows 3, 4 etc. until you come to the last row. You should end up with a gap into which you can pile the soil from the first trench. It is very important to then wait for about 4 to 6 weeks before you level the soil and make up the beds. If you try to do this too early you will pull out and expose the sods. You need to give them time to break down. After that you can prepare the beds as described above.

Example of single digging

18

Don't let the digging put you off though. It's not the easiest job, especially trying to turn over the sods properly so that the grass won't show. If you find it too tough, decide on an easier option.

Option 3: Making raised beds with timber sides

Anyone with even the most basic carpentry skills can make a raised bed. The big advantage of this system is that you don't have to dig provided the beds are a minimum of 20cm high. The most suitable timber for this purpose is untreated larch or cedar. They last quite well for a number of years even without wood treatment.

The big advantage of this system is that you don't even have to dig the plot over. You can simply place the raised bed over the grass.

It's a great way of converting your lawn into something more productive.

To fill a raised bed, simply lay out thick layers of newspaper (at least 7 sheets) or overlapping cardboard inside the bed onto the grass, making sure that the newspaper overlaps and covers the whole area.

Then, place a 5cm deep layer of composted manure on top of the newspaper, followed by a 15cm layer of good topsoil. You may be lucky enough to have spare topsoil in your garden and you could mix that with composted manure from a garden centre. Some counties have municipal composting facilities and you may be able to get some green-waste compost.

After you have filled the raised beds you should wait for a week for the soil to settle and then you are ready to sow or plant.

Example of a raised bed

Option 4: The No-Dig Garden

This method is an adaptation of the of the raised beds, but without the use of timber. Mark out the vegetable plot, strim or mow the area and cover with overlapping cardboard which is held down initially with a very thin layer of semi-decomposed wood-chips (no more than 2cm). Cover the entire area, e.g. 100m² for an outdoor vegetable garden. On top of the cardboard and wood chip, spread about 10cm of composted manure (horse or cattle). On top of the composted manure spread around 10cm of green-waste compost. This can be slightly rough or unscreened, and then finish off with 5cm of screened green-waste compost.

If you can get hold of some mushroom compost, you can use this instead of municipal green-waste compost. Ideally finish off with a 5cm layer of good topsoil. If the topsoil is poor, you can mix compost and soil together.

Let's take a 100m² plot for ease of calculations:
One cubic metre (m³) measures 1m x 1m x 1m. One cubic metre of composted manure spread at a depth of 10cm will reach 10m².

You would need 10m³ to cover 100m². You'll also need 10m³ of rough green-waste compost and finally 5m³ of screened green-waste compost.

This may work out quite expensive. The advantage is that after letting it all settle for a couple of weeks you can start planting.
If your soil is reasonably good, I would recommend **not** to use this system.
Instead, incorporate the compost or composted manure into your existing soil to further improve it. However, if your soil is very bad and too difficult to improve, I would recommend this system.

Option 5: Lazy beds

Lazy beds date back to the early 1800's. They were used by farmers in Ireland who were forced onto poor, boggy land where nothing would grow. Only with the use of lazy beds could they feed their livestock and families. Anyone who visits the West of Ireland can still see traces of this ancient cultivation technique which is so unique to Ireland. It is an ideal system of getting a crop out of a very poor and wet soil and secondly lazy beds provide us with an important historical link to the past.

I would love every Irish person to get the opportunity to have a try making a lazy bed once in their life. We will quickly appreciate that it is not a lazy task. It can be quite back-breaking work especially if we don't have adequate tools. At least we don't have to do half an acre of it.

Tools

Each county in Ireland seems to have developed a tool (Loy or McMahon spade) for turning the sods of the lazy beds.

How to make lazy beds?

1. You start off with a lawn. The better the lawn, the easier it will be to lift the sods.
2. Mark out the area and stretch garden lines sloping downwards three feet apart.
3. Place manure on one side of the line about 20cm wide and 5-10cm high. This is on top of the grass.

4. Put the seed potatoes on top of the manure, 25cm apart for earlies, 30cm apart for maincrops.
5. Place the garden line between the two bands of manure and cut the sod with a spade or edging tool.
6. Now comes the tough job. You cut under the sod and turn it onto the potatoes. When you finish the first line repeat this on the other side so the whole drill is covered with sods from either side.

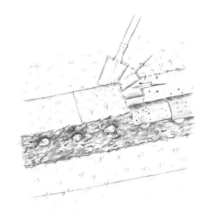

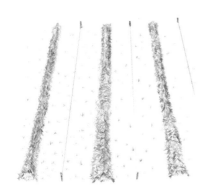

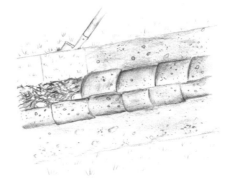

7. After that, you shovel some soil from the pathways onto the drills.

8. During the growing season earth up the potatoes once or twice.

9. Harvesting is definitely the best fun: You simply open up the sods (with strong hands and gloves) and the potatoes just lie there on top of the manure which has since decomposed nicely.

This is such an excellent method of ground preparation.
The following year you can top it up with some more compost and you can grow any other vegetable in it.

Option 6: Huegel bed

A Huegel bed is an old German tradition and certainly not for the faint-hearted.

I only ever made two Huegel beds. It is hard work but, apart from labour, there is no additional cost and on top of that they are brilliant for growing vegetables. To give you an idea – a 6m long and 1.8m wide Huegel bed took me a full day to build. It was certainly worth it, because 5 years after we still get great crops from it even though it has shrunk.

A Huegel bed is also a must for any climate change activist. What we are actually doing is burying carbon – putting carbon back into the soil where it belongs.

How to build a Huegel bed?

The base area is 1.8m wide and can be as long as you require. First, remove the sods and place aside, then dig out about 20cm of topsoil and place separately as well. You will need it later. The first layer consists of larger branches followed by smaller branches, herbaceous prunings etc. Start building the mound with these materials but only in the centre of the dug out part (80cm wide and 80cm high).

The second layer consists of the grass sods turned upside down on top of the woody materials.

The third layer is a 15cm layer of leaf mould. I didn't have leaf mould so I used fresh seaweed instead.

The fourth layer is a 15cm layer of good, semi-decomposed, farmyard manure with plenty of worms.

To finish, place a 20cm layer of soil (which was placed aside earlier and is thoroughly mixed with good compost).

The initial Huegel bed is over 1m tall, but will settle and shrink a little bit every year.

The benefits are manifold:

The surface area is increased and you'll achieve a much higher yield from a small area. As the materials decompose, heat is released and you'll get a free, underground heating system for a while.

You'll get better germination and earlier crops. You can possibly grow vegetables that won't grow naturally in Ireland. The drainage is massively improved.

There is enough soil fertility to last for three to four years. Then, you can simply top it up with garden compost.

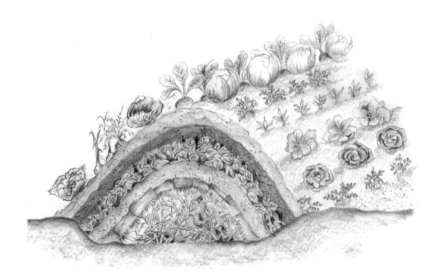

Composting

Good compost making is the key element of a productive, self-sufficient garden. The better your compost, the better your crops. But it is forgiving, even if we make many mistakes it will work out in the end as it is a natural process. Composting ensures that nutrients which have been taken out of the ground by our crops will return back into the soil.

Think about it philosophically - it is the end of a life cycle and at the same time the beginning of new life forms. It illustrates this everlasting cycle of dying and becoming.

It's the billions of microscopic creatures which we can't even see with our naked eyes that do all the work for us. In fact, in one handful of compost there are more living beings than there are people on Earth!

Composting – a climate solution?

Plants absorb (breathe in) carbon (a greenhouse gas and nutrient) from the atmosphere and when you compost the plants this carbon is partly going back to the soil in the form of organic matter or humus, which is quite safely stored in the soil for many years and some of it even for many decades. So, the most active way to counteract global warming is to compost every bit of waste.

Choosing a site

Your compost heaps should be placed at the most convenient location in your garden in full sun or semi-shade with easy access. It should sit directly on the soil allowing easy movement of organisms between the heap and the soil.

What can be composted?

In general, anything that was once alive can be composted. However, cooked food waste and meat leftovers can pose problems by attracting vermin. These could be initially composted in a fully enclosed wormery or tumbler compost. If you are planning for a completely self-sufficient garden, you are most likely bringing in raw materials from other sources for composting. Suitable materials include wood chips, fresh seaweed, horse manure, cattle manure, green waste compost and mushroom compost.

Composted wood chip

Semi-composted wood chip from a tree surgeon. This is generally a waste product and either free for collection or a minimal cost for delivery. Simply contact a tree surgeon and ask if there is an old pile of it sitting around. They are only happy to get rid of it. I have been using semi-composted wood chips a lot in recent years, both as a mulch but also to make paths between vegetable beds. I shovel out the soil from the paths (up to 20cm deep) and spread it onto the beds and then backfill the paths with semi-decomposed wood chips, then I let soil fall onto the paths.

This seems like a lot of work and I would only do it if I don't have enough topsoil and if the ground is too wet.

Fresh seaweed

Enjoy a trip to the coast and fill compost bags with washed up seaweed. It's an excellent addition to a compost heap

Horse and cattle manure

A layer of horse or cattle manure into your compost is the best compost activator.

Green waste compost

It's rare that a garden produces sufficient compost with its own ingredients. You may need to get in additional compost from a local municipal source.

Spent mushroom compost

Spent mushroom compost is an excellent soil conditioner and will massively improve the structure of your soil. Anyone who is certified organic will need to source an organically certified mushroom compost.

Leaf-mould

Collect as much leaf-mould as possible in the autumn and store it in a container (e.g. 4 fence posts surrounded with chicken wire) next to your compost bin.

The following year, it's ideal to layer it with lawn mowings in the New Zealand Box.

Choosing a compost bin

For a larger self-sufficient garden, I would recommend a 3 or even 4-bay New Zealand Box with an additional worm composting bin for cooked food waste.

New Zealand Box

This is definitely my favourite composting system. It consists of three equal-sized compartments. You always put the new material in the first compartment and when it is full you turn the contents from the first section into the middle compartment.

You can then start filling the first one again. When it is full again, turn the middle section into the third section and the first one into the second.

It is an absolute foolproof system and you can make brilliant compost in less than three months. It's definitely the best option if you have a reasonably sized garden.

The dimensions could be a minimum of 1.2m x 1.2m for each compartment with a height of at least 1.5m. Having a fourth or even fifth compartment will allow you to bring in and store manure, autumn leaves or wood chips. It can be designed in such a way that the timber on the front and sides of the compartments can be slid in to make filling and turning easier.

New Zealand Box

Worm composting bins (wormeries)

A completely different technique is the use of a wormery to produce compost. This method relies largely on worms to carry out decomposition and does not heat up during the process.

A wormery is a fully enclosed container which is usually comes with Tiger worms. The population of worms increases during the process. Wormeries are suitable for both indoor and outdoor use as they are totally enclosed. They produce top-quality compost often used in potting mixtures. They are also very popular with children!

A disadvantage of wormeries is that much more care is needed to ensure that the worms are fed correctly, otherwise the process may be slow or the worms may die. Wormeries come in a wide range of sizes and types.

How to make good compost

Here are a few tips to make great compost:

a) Use the right ingredients - getting the Brown and Green balance right

Making compost is a bit like baking a cake.

Composting ingredients can be divided into Green and Brown categories depending on their chemical make-up. In technical terms Green waste contains a high percentage of nitrogen and Brown waste a high percentage of carbon. As a rule, roughly equal amounts of each type of waste should be used. Most people find it difficult to gather enough Brown material for composting. A tip here is to gather a few sacks of autumn leaves for adding to your heap throughout the year. Wood chips are also a Brown material.

When starting a compost heap, first place a layer of brown material in your container. Straw, shredded twigs, paper or autumn leaves are ideal for this. Once this first layer has been placed in the container, the Green and Brown materials be added in alternate layers, 5cm to 10cm thick from then on. The more varied the ingredients you put into your heap, the better the compost you will make.

The most common problem is that too much kitchen waste and grass clippings are added without enough Brown material. This restricts movement of air, which slows down the process and may cause offensive odours.

Less frequently, problems can arise from the addition of too much Brown material. If too many leaves, shredded twigs and shredded hedge clippings are added, the composting process will be very slow.

A great compost recipe:

During the week, add garden waste, uncooked kitchen waste (at the correct green/brown ratio) into the pile and then, once per week, have your composting hour. Mow your lawn and collect one wheelbarrow full of lawn mowings and put it into your New Zealand Box. On top of that put in one wheelbarrow full of either old leaves (collected from previous autumn and stored conveniently) or semi-composted wood chips.

The final wheelbarrow is either horse or cattle manure. For a smaller compost you may only need a bucket of each of the above.

This could be your weekly composting exercise – no need for a gym!

Aim to fill the compartment as quickly as possible. Once full turn it into the second compartment and fill the first one again.

Then, turn the second into the third compartment and the first into the second and so on.

You will be able to have the best compost ready within 10 to 12 weeks if you get enough material. How satisfying is that?

Green materials (activators):

Grass cuttings
Young weeds
Poultry manure
Comfrey leaves
Fresh seaweed

Neutral materials:

Kitchen scraps
Vegetable peelings
Tea leaves
Coffee grinds
Fruit peelings
Animal manures from sheep, cattle, horses, rabbits)

Brown materials (slow to rot):

Egg shells
Wood ash
Sawdust and wood shavings
Small amounts of soil
Small hedge clippings (shredded)
Autumn leaves
Old plants
Small quantities of paper (torn up or shredded)
Straw
Hay

Do not add to your compost:
Meat, chicken and fish leftovers
Manure from meat eating animals, such as dogs and cats
Certain weed roots especially bindweed, ground elder, scutch grass
Coal ashes
Glossy magazines
Large woody material
Chemically treated garden waste
Animal carcasses
Disposable nappies

b) The right moisture content - not too wet and not too dry
It is important that your compost heap is not too wet and not too dry. If too much wet material such as coffee grinds, tea leaves etc. is added, it will restrict the amount of air in the heap, slow down the process and may lead to offensive odours. As Ireland has high rainfall, it is very important to ensure that your heap is protected from the rain.
A less common problem is a compost heap that is too dry. In this case composting will be very slow as micro-organisms need moisture to work efficiently. Simply watering the heap should cure the problem. Microorganisms generally thrive in a well-aerated environment and so a heap which has plenty of air is much more efficient.

c) Chop or shred materials if possible
Smaller particles of material are more quickly and easily broken down. For example, a cabbage stalk, if added directly to a heap, may take up to two years to break down fully. However, if shredded or chopped in small pieces, the same stalk will be fully composted within a few months.

How do I know when my compost is ready?

The aim of composting is to turn household and garden waste into a sweet smelling, crumbly and dark brown compost which will feed both the soil and the plants you grow the following year.

After having turned the compost twice, you'll know when your compost is ready. Crumble it through your fingers and it should be dark, crumbly and sweet-smelling – just like buttery, black gold.
Don't be put off if there are a few woody branches or egg shells which are not fully decomposed. Home-produced compost will not typically be as fine as bagged compost available from a garden centre.

There is no harm in spreading these semi-composted twigs into the garden or if you prefer you could move them through the composting system again.

How to use your compost?

Mulching:
Spread a layer of about two inches of compost around plants on ground that has been cleared of weeds. The mulch will suppress new weed growth, improve the soil and hold moisture. This should only be done when the soil has warmed up.

Soil improver:
Work compost into your soil to enrich it. When using compost in this way there is no need to sieve the compost as leaving some smaller twigs etc. may even benefit your soil.

Potting mixes:
To make shop-bought compost go further, add up to 50% of your own compost which has been sieved and mix thoroughly. To make your own potting compost use one part sieved compost, one part sharp sand and one part finely sieved soil and mix well.

Propagation

Sowing

For a self-sufficient garden you will need a small propagation greenhouse or a propagation space in your polytunnel.

For the smaller garden, a small propagation area with a heating bench of about 0.5m² may be sufficient. For the complete self-sufficient garden, the propagation area would need to be at least 4m² with a heating bench about 2m².

With a heating bench/propagator you can start sowing from January onwards, thus extending the growing season.

Greenhouses, with their higher light transmission, are better for propagation, especially very early in the year where every ray of sunlight is so important to prevent your seedlings from getting too leggy. Polytunnels are second best but also possible. Make sure that the plastic is clean.

Most vegetables are sown from seed. Only some are planted as sets (onions, shallots) and some as tubers (potatoes and Jerusalem artichokes).

Seeds

For successful germination you need viable seeds. Seeds will deteriorate in storage.

On average, seeds store for 2-4 years in a cool, dry place. Parsnip and celery seeds, however, last only for one season. Seeds should never be left in a hot or damp polytunnel as they will deteriorate quickly.

Correct temperature for germination

Each crop has got its minimum, optimum and maximum temperature for germination.

Generally, the higher the temperature, the better the germination.

On the other hand, too high a temperature can be detrimental (e.g. lettuce does not germinate well above 25°C). A good average temperature for most crops would be about 18 - 19°C and 20 - 23°C for tomatoes, peppers and cucumbers.

There are different types of heated propagation units:
- Heating bench with electric cables on sand and thermostat.
- Heating mat with thermostat.
- Electrical propagators (purpose-built)

Propagation area

Crop	Germination Temperature in °C			Days to germination under optimum temperature and moisture conditions
	Min	Opt	Max	
Beetroot	8	28	33	6
Broccoli	7	25	30	4
Brussels sprouts	6	30	33	4
Cabbage	10	30	35	4
Carrot	7	25	30	8
Cauliflower	8	23	30	5
Celery	15	20	24	7
Cucumber	20	30	35	3
Kale	10	32	37	4
Leek	8	25	30	7
Lettuce	7	18	23	3
Onion	10	23	33	7
Parsley	10	23	30	13
Parsnip	10	17	20	14
Pea	15	23	27	6
Pepper	18	30	37	8
Tomato	5	27	33	6
Turnip	15	30	38	3

Moisture and air

Seeds need moisture and air to germinate. The higher the temperature the higher the water uptake will be. If there is too much water in the seed compost the seeds may just rot away. Some composts have poorer drainage, especially soil-based composts and need to be watered more carefully.

Light

A few vegetable seeds require light to germinate, e.g. lettuce, celery and you shouldn't cover these seeds with compost, just place them on the surface. As soon as plants have germinated, they all require light to photo-synthesise. In winter and early spring, the natural light levels are quite low, so artificial light may be necessary to prevent plants from becoming leggy.

Storing seeds

Most vegetable seeds will keep easily for the next growing season provided they are kept cool and dry. Never leave seed packets outside in the garden, in a polytunnel or in a damp shed or garage, because the high humidity will quickly ruin them. An airtight glass jar or a ziploc bag is an ideal storage container.

They should ideally be kept in your coolest room, or better still, in a fridge. Apart from parsnips and celery, I use started seed packets for a second year and then buy new seeds. I'm aware that many seeds will keep for much longer, but I find that the vigour of the plants decreases with age and thus the quality of vegetables will decrease as well.

Sowing Methods

In theory, all vegetables can be sown directly into the ground where they are to grow, and thinned out to their final spacing. However, raising plants indoors and transplanting them out has many advantages for a number of crops.

Direct Sowing

When sowing seeds directly into the soil, ensure that the soil has a loose and friable structure with a fine seedbed. Root crops, such as carrots and parsnips, need to be sown directly into the ground. If they are sown in modules their tap roots get air-pruned and the roots will start to spiral around in the module. They will never form proper carrots or parsnip and will continue to twist and turn in the soil.

Other root crops such as swedes, turnips and radishes can either be sown directly into the soil or raised in modular trays.

Also vegetables with large seeds such as peas and beans are generally sown directly into the soil but mainly to save space in the propagation house.

Most other vegetables will perform much better if they are raised indoors and planted out at a later stage.

Seedbed preparation and sowing
In early spring, after the initial ground preparation rake the beds every two weeks. After each raking, a new flush of weed seedlings will appear and will be controlled again at the next raking. The method is called the stale seedbed method or false seedbed technique and is by far the most efficient method of weed control.

By the time you sow your crops you'll have a great seedbed with a fine tilth.
Mark the drill lines with a tight string and make a seed drill using an onion (round hoe). The depth of the furrow depends on the type of vegetable.

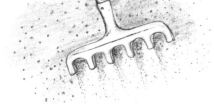

Then sprinkle the seeds thinly into the drill. With small seeds (e.g. carrot seeds), hold a pinch of about 50 seeds between your thumb and forefinger and release the seeds slowly. You can practice first on a table. Sow thinly to minimise thinning and to save on seeds. Larger seeds (e.g. beetroot and parsnip) can be sown individually.

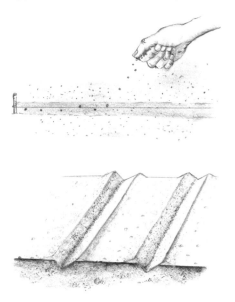

After sowing the seeds in the bed, rake over diagonally to close in the seeds.

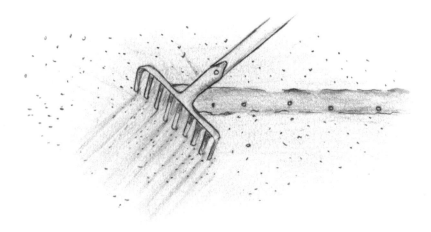

Then tap lightly with the rake to gently firm in the seeds. Water if the soil is very dry. Soon after the seedlings have germinated you may need to thin them out. If the seedlings are too crowded you'll have very small crops.

Heating bench
A heating bench with a thermostat is necessary for a self-sufficient garden. You can either opt for a heating bench with soil-warming cables or a heating mat.

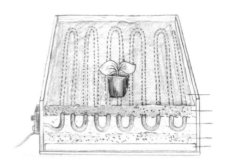

Indoor Sowing

A small greenhouse or a space in the polytunnel is ideal for starting off seedlings. This should be well designed and will be the centre of your activities. The alternative is a south-facing windowsill in the house.

The process from sowing to planting may take about 4 - 8 weeks depending on the season and the crop. Many vegetables benefit from transplanting because they are easier and quicker to germinate with extra care and warmth, and they will be weeks ahead of the weeds.

Sowing into modular trays:
The most common method is sowing seeds directly into modular trays. The main advantage is that there is no root disturbance when planting out. Fill the tray with a good seed compost which is usually quite fine, tap the tray on the table to firm in the compost, fill again and level off any excess compost.

Then, make a fingernail deep indentation in the centre of the module. This is an easy general guideline for most vegetables.

The smaller the seeds, the shallower the sowing depth, and remember for lettuce and celery sow on top and do not cover the seeds.

Larger seeds (e.g. spinach, beetroot) can be sown by hand while smaller seeds are placed on a folded piece of paper and scraped into the holes using a pencil.

My favourite modular tray is a good quality 77 cell tray – the make I have is Quickpot and they should last for a decade.

Sowing into standards seed trays or pots:
Some seeds are best broadcast-sown into pots or standard seed trays. These include vegetables with tiny seeds (celery and celeriac) and vegetables that take a long time to germinate (tomatoes, peppers and aubergines). I start off fast growing plants like courgette, squash and cucumbers in 7cm pots.

Pricking out

If the seeds were broadcast-sown in standard seed trays or pots, they need to be pricked out at an early stage before the roots become too entangled – about a week or two after germination. Some vegetables will be pricked out into modular trays (celery and celeriac) and others into small pots (tomatoes, peppers and aubergines).

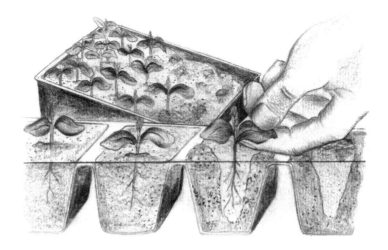

At this stage, a more nutrient-rich potting compost is used. Always hold the seedling on the seed leaf (cotyledon) and ease the roots out with a small stick or label.

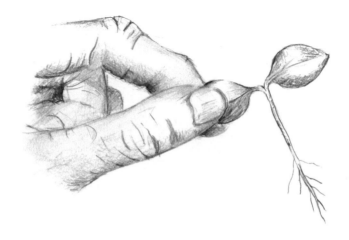

If the seedlings have become leggy or drawn, this means that they didn't get sufficient light. This often happens very early in the year or when they are raised on the windowsill.

This can be remedied by planting the seedling deeper. Simply bury the leggy stem (hypocotyls) right up to the seed leaves.

Hardening off

It is essential that all plants that are raised indoors are acclimatised before they are planted outside. Traditionally the seedling trays were moved outdoors during the day and then returned to the greenhouse.

Alternatively, the trays could be moved into a coldframe with either a glass polycarbonate or plastic lid for a week before planting out. The lid is opened during the day and closed at night.

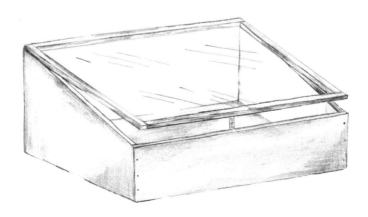

The easiest method for hardening off plants is with the help of a bionet cloche. You can plant out seedlings directly from the greenhouse into the open ground and place the mobile bionet cloche over the crop for a week.

Bionet cloche

Transplant out when plants are ready. Don't let your transplants get pot-bound in the modules. Modular transplants should be planted as soon as the root ball comes out easily without the compost falling off it.

Transplants should be planted quite firmly into the soil so there is good contact between the roots and the soil. Most beginners compact the soil above, rather than pushing the transplant in.

The best time of day to plant out is during dull weather in the evening. If you plant out your seedlings in the morning on a beautiful, hot, sunny day they are likely to wilt due to extensive evaporation. This applies only during the warmer periods.

The most efficient way for plant arrangement is to plant at equidistant (or staggered) spacing.

Rotation

If crops are grown continuously on the same piece of land the soil will sooner or later become exhausted. In some fertile areas throughout the world this ancient knowledge was neglected and the same crops are grown on the same piece of land for up to 40 years. There are fields in Ireland where only barley has grown in the last number of decades, artificially kept alive with synthetic fertilisers, pesticides and weedkillers. This is not how nature intended it.

Nature also occasionally needs a rest. In old farming traditions a fallow period was included in the rotation which allowed weeds to grow and replenish the soil. A gardener can now use a mixed green manure for this purpose.

What is a crop rotation?

The principle of crop rotation is to group related vegetables together and move them around your garden so that they do not grow on the same plot for a number of years.

Benefits of crop rotations?

Pest and disease control:
Pest and disease pathogens can build up to catastrophic levels if the same host crops are grown on the same spot year after year. If you move your crops around you interrupt the cycles of those pests and diseases.

However, a crop rotation is not the cure for all pests and diseases. Rotation is only effective for **soil-borne** pests and diseases that are specific to a particular plant family.

Do you think a slug minds if it has a lettuce or a radish for breakfast? The carrot fly will find your carrots no matter where they are in your garden.

However, a rotation is absolutely essential in limiting the spread of the following soil-borne pests and diseases:
- Clubroot on brassicas (cabbage family)
- Nematodes on potatoes
- White rot on alliums (onion family)

Soil fertility:
Vegetables differ in what they take out of the soil and what they give back to it. If you include peas and beans in your rotation they will add nitrogen to the soil. A leguminous green manure in your rotation will add even more.

Soil structure:
A well-designed rotation can help in improving the structure of your soil. Some crops have a very deep taproot which can penetrate into the subsoil and extract nutrients from low down. Thus, you should alternate deep-rooting vegetables (or green manures) with shallow rooting ones.

Weed control:
If you alternate weed susceptible crops such as onions with weed suppressing crops such as potatoes or cabbages, the weed problems for the susceptible crops may be lessened.

Length of rotation

A three-year rotation is the absolute minimum, and suitable if you have only three beds available. The longer the rotation is, the more benefits you get from it.
A four-year rotation is usually sufficient and easily managed. If it suits your needs, you can have a much longer rotation.

Planning a rotation

1. Make a list of all the vegetables you want to grow. Don't include perennial crops, such as asparagus or rhubarb in this list. Perennial vegetables have to be grown in a permanent plot.
2. Group the vegetables into plant families.
3. Divide up the garden into equal plots (3, 4 or 5 plots) .
4. Decide which families will be grouped together. You will notice that there are more than four vegetable families. The families should be suited to each other. For example, the carrot and onion family is very compatible because they have similar growth habits.
5. Draw up a plan.

Vegetable families

Brassicaceae (Cabbage family)
Brussels sprouts
Broccoli
Cabbage
Calabrese
Cauliflower
Kale

Kohlrabi
Pak choi
Rocket
Radish
Swede
Turnip

Leguminosae (Pea family)
Pea
Bean
Clovers

Solanaceae (Potato family)
Aubergine (polytunnel only)
Pepper (polytunnel only)
Potato
Tomato (polytunnel only)

Apiaceae or Umbelliferae (Carrot family)
Carrot
Celeriac
Celery
Florence fennel
Parsnips
Annual herbs: dill, coriander, chervil, parsley

Compositae (Daisy family)
Cardoon (perennial)
Chicory
Endive
Jerusalem artichoke (grown as perennial)
Globe artichoke (perennial)
Lettuce
Salsify
Scorzonera

Alliaceae (Onion family)
Garlic
Leek
Onion
Scallion
Shallot

Chenopodiaceae (Beetroot family)
Beetroot
Chard
Spinach

Cucurbitaceae (Cucumber family)
Courgette
Cucumber (polytunnel only)
Marrow
Pumpkin
Squash

Unrelated vegetables
Sweetcorn (Gramineae)
Corn salad (Valerianaceae)
Winter purslane (Portulaceae)
Asparagus (Asparagaceae)

Mixed Cropping

Mixed Planting - Intercropping

Intercropping or interplanting are alternative words for companion planting, but there is no claim that one particular plant will harm or benefit a neighbouring plant, unless it is scientifically proven. It is an excellent way of maximising your garden space and just the fact that there is a much greater plant diversity, there is probably less likelihood of pests and diseases getting out of hand.

In a self-sufficient garden there is so much scope for intercropping and it can easily increase your yields by half or even double. It requires some planning and forward thinking, but it's great fun.

There are various ways for mixing vegetables in a bed:

Row intercropping

You can grow a different vegetable in each row in the same bed. For example, instead of having four rows of parsnips in a single bed you could sow alternate rows of parsnips and beetroot. Another combination could be alternate rows of lettuce and annual spinach or kale and rainbow chard.

Mixed intercropping

Grow a number of different vegetables in the same bed at random or even in mixed patterns. This can have a beautiful effect and makes gardening fun. If the plants are not in rows, hoeing will be more difficult and you may need to hand-weed the beds. It's important that the crops you choose are compatible. There is plenty of scope for experimenting. For some more excellent guidance and information refer to Joy Larkcom's wonderful book:
Creative Vegetable Gardening.

Relay intercropping

You can plant fast growing and quick maturing crops in between the slower growing and more widely spaced crops. For example, you can plant lettuce, annual spinach, oriental salads or radish between kale, sprouting broccoli and Brussels sprouts. The fast growing crops will be harvested before the bigger plants need that space.

Intersowing

I'm not sure if this term exists, but you can mix vegetable seeds which germinate and mature quickly with vegetables that germinate slowly and also mature more slowly. The best example is to mix a few radish seeds in with your carrot or parsnip seeds. The radishes will germinate very quickly and show you where the row is so you can hoe. The radishes can be harvested well before the carrots need that space.

Catch cropping

Quite often our garden beds are bare for prolonged periods of time. Catch cropping refers to making use of the ground either before or after it is needed by the maincrop. For example, early potatoes may be harvested in July and they can be followed by a catch crop of turnips, Chinese cabbage, Florence fennel or oriental salads. Also late planted crops such as kale, Brussels sprouts, leeks and purple sprouting broccoli can be preceded by a quick maturing catch crop such as lettuce, radish, turnip, annual spinach or oriental salads.

Wild Interplanting

Dr. Christine Jones inspired me to come up with this idea. Her research focuses on diverse cover crop mixtures for farms and with massive improvements on soil fertility and resilience to adverse weather conditions.

Here is my interpretation for vegetable crop mixtures:

I mix 15 different vegetables, salad and annual herb seeds together and multi-sow (5 seed/cell) the seeds in April into modular trays. A month later, they are planted out about 25cm apart each way, at random in the Huegelbed, or in rows in a raised bed.

As the plants grow, thin them out and eat the thinnings or small vegetables. The fast-maturing crops such as dill, coriander and radishes are eaten first, then the salads and lettuces and at the end of the season you are left with the kales, cabbages and chards.

This is a more labour-intensive system but a lot more productive. I also found that all the crops grew a lot healthier.

Keep harvesting throughout the season, otherwise it will be too crowded and production suffers.

I would use the following crops in this mixture – red cabbage, kale, rainbow chard, scallions, lettuce (3 types), rocket, mizuna, tatsoi, radish, beetroot, dill, coriander, chervil. It requires some gardening knowledge to identify all the plants at different development stages – there is always something new to learn.

Examples of fast growing vegetables which are suitable for planting in between slower crops:

Lettuce - especially loose-leafed types or dwarf varieties.

Radishes – but remember they are in the brassica family so be careful not to confuse your rotation.

Turnips – they are also brassicas and only suitable when grown with other brassicas.

Oriental salads – excellent for intercropping as they can be harvested at any stage – brassica family.

Annual spinach – one of the best intercrops as you can harvest it even at the baby leaf stage. The biggest benefit is that it is not susceptible to any specific soil-borne pest or disease, so you don't have to worry about your rotation. It's a very flexible crop.

Examples of slow growing vegetables which can be inter-cropped at their early stages:
Brussels sprouts
Kale
Sprouting broccoli
Sweetcorn

Important tips:

Spacing:
It may seem obvious, but it deserves a mention: intercropping doesn't give you an excuse to cram plants together. For example, if you intercrop parsnips and beetroot, you can't just sow beetroot between two rows of parsnips. You have to substitute one row of parsnips for beetroot.

Shading:
When you mix vegetables, select them carefully to avoid shading and excessive competition for water and nutrients. Once you start experimenting, you can have lots of fun and make more discoveries.

Mixed cropping.

Row intercropping

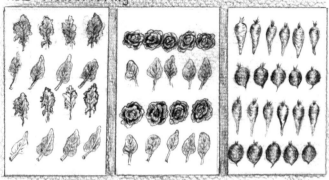

Kale + rainbow chard   lettuce + annual spinach   Parsnip + beetroot

Mixed intercropping

Spinach + lettuce + cabbage + kale + celery + beetroot

Relay intercropping

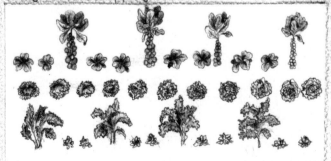

Brussels sprouts   kale + fast growing crops

Intersowing

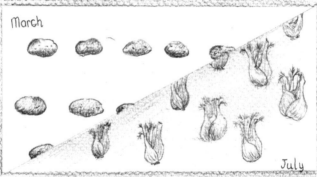

Parsnip + radish

Catch cropping

March

July

Potatoes · fennel

Wild interplanting

Planning a self-sufficient garden

Every garden has its own characteristics and every family has its own preferences of what they would like to grow and eat. The more gardening experience you have, the more you manage to cultivate, in less time. For new gardeners, the best advice is to start small. It is very discouraging to plant more than you can look after and then the pleasure may turn into a chore.

The size you choose depends entirely on you, on your skills, fitness, motivation, the size of your garden and your knowledge of vegetable growing. I would strongly recommend not to take on too much in the first year, but to plan your plot in such a way that you can extend it in the future.

On the other hand, there are people who simply jump right into it and manage to produce nearly all their food from their own garden.

You will be surprised how much produce you will get out of a small plot of land. Hardly a day will pass without getting a fresh salad out of your garden.

In the following pages, I will outline three crop plans which I hope you'll find useful. You can easily adjust them to suit your own needs. I also discuss different methods of crop planning – with little planning for the small garden, a more detailed plan for the 100m² garden and a very detailed plan for the complete self-sufficient garden.
There is a drawing, followed by a cropping plan and then a sowing plan.
The sowing plan is the handiest and the only plan you'll need to remind you what and when to sow, and where it will go.

Overview of crop plans:

A. Crop plan for high value crops (50m² outdoor garden).

B. Crop plan for staple crops (100m² outdoor garden).

C. Crop plan for complete self-sufficiency from a 300m² outdoor garden and 90m² polytunnel.

How much time do I need to grow my own vegetables?

The amount of time you need to spend to prepare the soil and tend the crops depends on a number of factors. In spring you are busy with soil preparation, sowing, planting and caring for your crops until they fill out the beds and weed growth slows down. In summer there is much less to do apart from the occasional weeding and hoeing.

For the complete self-sufficient garden you may need about 20 hours per week on average – this could be a couple working together on a Saturday and an additional half an hour most evenings. There will be much less time needed for the smaller gardens.

If you do the right job at the right time, and do it properly, you can save yourself hours of unnecessary work.

A.   Crop plan for high-value crops in small garden

This garden is designed to produce the highest value crops from a small space.   It's all fresh produce that requires regular maintenance and harvesting, so this garden should be close to your house.   This can be easily adapted according to your own requirements.   For example, if you juice kale, chard and celery you could grow a lot more of it.
The size of this sample garden is 6.8m x 7.2m (52m²).

You can easily change a few crops around and include more crops that need regular maintenance.   Lettuce and annual spinach can be planted into gaps between wider spaced crops, or it could be planted before a late planted vegetable or after a crop that will be harvested in early summer. Both lettuce and annual spinach are very useful for this purpose and you don't need to worry where they fit in the rotation as they are neutral crops.

Rotation:
Beds 1 & 2 Cabbage Family
Beds 3 & 4 Carrot & Onion Family
Beds 5 & 6 Legume & Cucurbit Family
Beds 7 & 8 Beet Family

You can rotate the two beds together – for example Beds 1 & 2 follow Beds 3 & 4.

CROP PLAN FOR HIGH-VALUE
CROPS IN A SMALL GARDEN

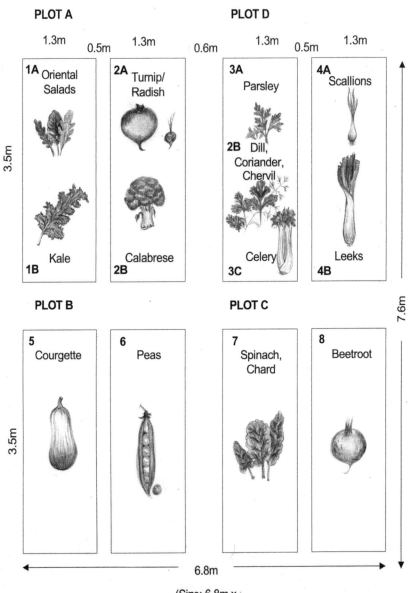

PLOT A

1.3m   0.5m   1.3m   0.6m

3.5m

1A Oriental Salads

2A Turnip/ Radish

Kale
1B

Calabrese
2B

PLOT D

1.3m   0.5m   1.3m

3A Parsley

2B Dill, Coriander, Chervil

Celery
3C

4A Scallions

Leeks
4B

7.6m

PLOT B

3.5m

5 Courgette

6 Peas

PLOT C

7 Spinach, Chard

8 Beetroot

6.8m

(Size: 6.8m x 7.6m = 52m²)

Bed 1a: Oriental salads (1.5m)
Sow in succession whenever required.
Bed 1b: Kale (2m)
Sow 6 kale plants in mid-April and 6 kale plants in mid-June, plant 4 weeks later.
Bed 2a: Radish/turnip (1.5m)
Sow in succession whenever required.
Bed 2b: Calabrese (2m)
Sow 6 calabrese plants in mid-April and 6 calabrese plants in early June, plant 4 weeks later.
Bed 3a: Parsley (0.5m)
Sow 12 parsley plants (multi-sown @ 4 seeds/cell) in mid-April, plant out 4 weeks later.
Bed 3b: Dill, Coriander and Chervil (1.5m)
Sow in succession whenever required (April onwards).
Bed 3c: Celery (1.5m)
Sow 8 celery plants in mid-March, mid-April and mid-May, plant 7 weeks later.
Bed 4a: Scallions (1.5m)
Sow 8 scallion plants (10seeds/cell) in late March, late April and late May, plant 4 weeks later.
Bed 4b: Leeks (2m)
Sow 36 leek plants in mid-February and plant out later.
Bed 5:   Courgette (3.5m)
Sow 4 courgette plants in late April and plant in early June.
Bed 6:   Peas (3.5m)
Sow pea seeds directly into the ground in mid-April and again in mid-June.
Bed 7:   Perpetual spinach & chard (3.5m)
Sow 15 spinach/chard seeds in mid-April and again in mid-June and plant out 4 weeks later.
Bed 8:   Beetroot (3.5m)
Sow 4 rows of beetroot directly into the ground in late April.

B. Crop plan for a garden producing staple crops

This garden is highly productive and is suitable for gardeners who have little time available. It would be sufficient to work 4 to 5 hours per week on this garden and an additional few full days in spring to get the garden ready. The following crops are easy to grow and can be sown or planted in a few weekends, and after that there is very little maintenance required, apart from weeding and harvesting.

The size of this garden is 15m x 5m (125m²). The net growing area is 100m². You will be surprised how much produce you'll get from such a small space and it's a first step to self-sufficiency. It's also possible to combine it with Plan A which can be located closer to your house.

From this plot you could get over 300kg of vegetables.

Plot	Bed	Crop	Qty	Area	Yield/kg	Yield/No
A	1	Garlic	8 bulbs	5m	6	80 bulbs
A	2	Leeks	90 pl	5m	40	90 leeks
A	3	Onion	200 sets	5m	20	200 onion
B	1	Cabbage	18 pl	3m	25	18 heads
B	1	Kale	12	2m	10	200 leaves
B	2	Swede	120 pl	5m	30	120 swedes
B	3	Squashes	3 pl	5m	15	10 squash
C	1	Potato	64 tubers	5m	20	150 pots
C	2	Potato	48 tubers	5m	35	200 pots
C	3	Potato	48 tubers	5m	35	200 pots
D	1	Carrots	2 packs	5m	30	300
D	2	Parsnip	2 packs	5m	35	100 roots
D	3	Beetroot	2 packs	5m	15	200 roots

CROP PLAN FOR A GARDEN PRODUCING STAPLE CROPS

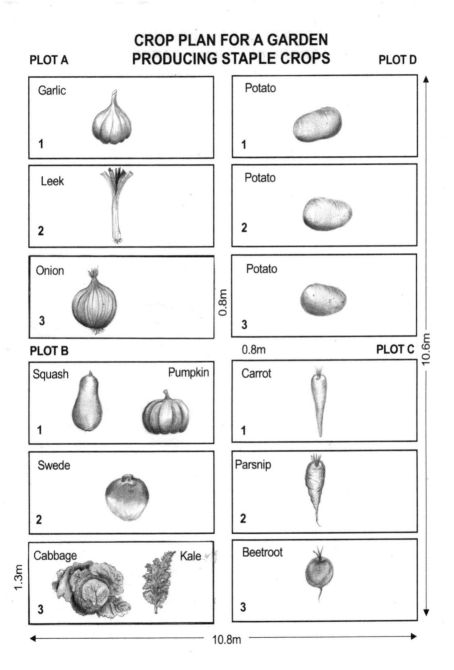

(Size: 10.8m x 10.8m=114.5m²)

Plot A:

1. Garlic

Planting: October – November or February- March

Spacing: 4 rows – 25cm between plants

Qty: 16 garlic cloves per m² x 5m/bed = 80 garlic cloves - @ 8 cloves per bulb

Requirement: 10 garlic bulbs for planting

2. Leeks

Grow a mixture of autumn (Hannibal) and winter (Bluegreen winter) leeks.

Sowing: mid-February to mid-March

Planting: April/May

Spacing: 3 rows – 15cm between plants

Qty: 20 leeks per m² x 5m/bed

Requirements: 100 leek plants

3. Onion

Grow a mixture of white and red onions

Planting: mid-March (brown types) to mid-April (red types)

Spacing: 4 rows – 10cm between plants

Qty: 40 onions per m² x 5m/bed = 200 onions

Plot B:

1. Cabbages (3m/bed) & Kale (2m/bed)

Ideally, choose different varieties with different maturity times – autumn and winter types.

Sowing: mid-April/mid-May

Spacing: 2 rows - 50cm between plants

Qty: 4 plants per m² x 5m = 20 plants

2. Swede

Two sowings of swedes, one in mid-April and one in early June will extend the harvesting time substantially.

Spacing: 4 rows – 20cm between plants

Qty: 20 swedes per m² x 5 = 100 swedes

3. Squash & Pumpkin

Sowing: late April in small pots indoors

Planting: late May/early June

Spacing: 1.5m between plants

Qty: 3 plants per 5m² = 3 plants

Plot C:
1. Carrot – maincrop (Romance F1, Autumn King)
Sowing: late May/early June directly into the soil
Spacing: 4 rows - 5cm between plants
Qty: 80 carrots per m² x 5m/bed = 400 carrots
2. Parsnip
Sowing: mid-April/early May directly into the soil
Spacing: 4 rows – 15cm between plants
Qty: 28 parsnip per m² x 5m/bed = 140 parsnips
3. Beetroot – maincrop
Sowing: early May/early June directly into the soil
Spacing: 4 rows – 10cm between plants
Qty: 40 beetroot per m² x 5m/bed = 200 beetroot

Plot D:
1. Potato – first early (e.g. Red Duke of York)
Twin row in bed – plant in mid-March
Spacing: 2 rows – 25cm (8 tubers per m²)
Qty: 8 tubers per m² x 5 = 40 potato tubers @ 10 tubers/kg
Requirements: 4kg seed potatoes
2. Potato – second early (e.g. Orla)
Twin row in bed – plant in late March
Spacing: 2 rows – 33cm (6 tubers per m²)
Qty: 6 tubers per m² x 5 = 30 potato tubers @ 10 tubers/kg
Requirements: 3kg seed potatoes
3. Potato – maincrop (e.g. Carolus)
Twin row in bed – plant in mid-April
Spacing: 2 rows – 33cm (6 tubers per m²)
Qty: 6 tubers per m² x 5 = 30 potato tubers @ 10 tubers/kg
Requirements: 3kg seed potatoes

NOTES:

C. Crop plan for a completely self-sufficient vegetable garden

The following plan is based on complete self-sufficiency in the majority of vegetables, for as many months as it is possible in this climate. Whenever suitable, the vegetables are grown outdoors and the season is extended both earlier and later with the help of a polytunnel.

The outdoor garden has a 5-year crop rotation and there are also a few beds for permanent crops (Jerusalem artichokes, strawberries and rhubarb). You could also add asparagus or any other perennial crops.

There are two polytunnel plans, one for the winter/spring period and the second for summer/autumn cropping. You'll find a few gaps which I called "flexicrops". I'm sure there are some crops you want to grow more of or, alternatively, experiment with some unusual crops such as the cucamelon or sweet potatoes. Asparagus grows best in a polytunnel with little or no watering so you may find a corner for this also.

The dimensions of this garden are around 400m² growing area. This is 300m² outdoor garden and a polytunnel just under 100m².

This is a more serious undertaking and will require some more gardening skills and time. The first year or two is always the hardest and as time goes on you'll figure out many labour saving techniques.

Don't forget your garden will be a special place for yourself, your family and all the plants and animals that choose to live there. Take some time out when you are in the garden to reflect on this beautiful ecosystem to which we all belong.

Crop plan for a Complete Self-Sufficient Garden

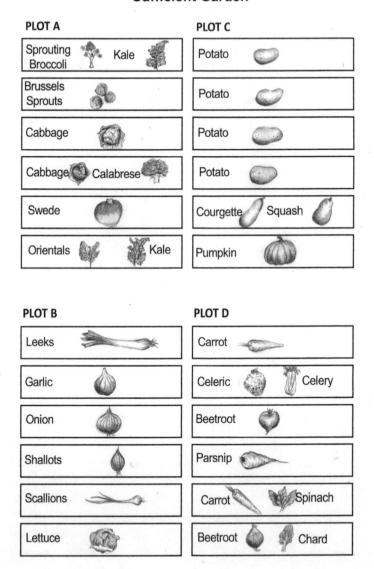

PLOT A

Sprouting Broccoli	Kale
Brussels Sprouts	
Cabbage	
Cabbage	Calabrese
Swede	
Orientals	Kale

PLOT C

| Potato |
| Potato |
| Potato |
| Potato |
| Courgette | Squash |
| Pumpkin |

PLOT B

| Leeks |
| Garlic |
| Onion |
| Shallots |
| Scallions |
| Lettuce |

PLOT D

| Carrot |
| Celeriac | Celery |
| Beetroot |
| Parsnip |
| Carrot | Spinach |
| Beetroot | Chard |

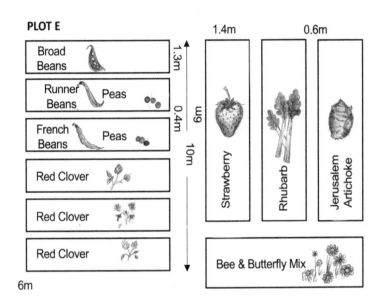

PLOT E

Broad Beans

Runner Beans | Peas

French Beans | Peas

Red Clover

Red Clover

Red Clover

1.3m

0.4m

6m

10m

6m

1.4m

0.6m

Strawberry

Rhubarb

Jerusalem Artichoke

Bee & Butterfly Mix

6m

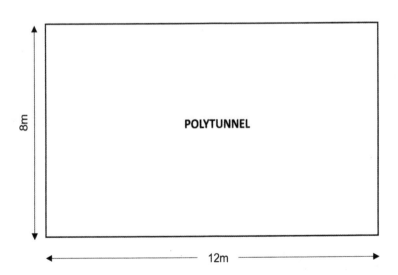

POLYTUNNEL

8m

12m

Crop plan for complete self-sufficient garden (outdoors)

Plot	Bed	Crop	Variety	Sowing	Sds/cell
A	1	Kale	various	05-Apr	1
A	1	Broccoli, Spr	Mixed	25- Jun	1
A	1	Kale	various	28-Apr	1
A	2	Br sprouts	Brigitte F1	24-Apr	1
A	2	Br sprouts	Brigitte F1	15-Jun	1
A	3	Cabbage	Stonehead F1	01-Apr	1
A	3	Cabbage	Rodynda	25-Apr	1
A	3	Cabbage	January King	20-May	1
A	4	Cabbage	Vertus	20-May	1
A	4	Calabrese	Chevalier F1	20-Mar	1
A	4	Calabrese	Chevalier F1	20-Apr	1
A	4	Calabrese	Chevalier F1	20-May	1
A	4	Calabrese	Chevalier F1	15-Jun	1
A	5	Swede	Gowrie	25-May	1
A	6	Kale	various	03-Jun	1
A	6	Oriental Salads	various	15-Jun	5
A	6	Oriental Salads	various	15-Jul	5
A	6	Oriental Salads	various	15-Aug	5
A	6	Turnip/Swede	mixed	15-Apr	1

Qty	Planting	Harvest	Clearing	Area	Spacing cm
6 pl	05-May	July	Sep	1m	45 x 45
6 pl	25 – Jul	Feb	May	4m	75 x 75
6 pl	28-May	Aug	Nov	1m	45 x 45
1 pack	24-May	Oct	Dec	3m	90 x 90
1 pack	15-Jul	Dec	Feb	3m	90 x 90
12 pl	01-May	July	Sep	2m	40 x 40
12 pl	25-May	Sep	Nov	2m	45 x 45
12 pl	20-Jun	Oct	Jan	2m	45 x 45
12 pl	20-Jun	Nov	Feb	2m	45 x 45
6 pl	20-Apr	June	July	1m	45 x 45
6 pl	20-May	July	Aug	1m	45 x 45
6 pl	20-Jun	Aug	Sep	1m	45 x 45
6 pl	15-Jun	Sep	Oct	1m	45 x 45
120pl	25-Jun	Oct	Nov	5m	20 x 30
6 pl	03-Jul	Oct	Feb	1m	45 x 45
16 pl	15-Jul	Aug	Sep	1m	20 x 25
16 pl	15-Aug	Sep	Feb	1m	20 x 25
16 pl	15-Sep	Oct	Feb	1m	20 x 25
72 pl	15-May	July	Sep	3m	15 x 25

Plot	Bed	Crop	Variety	Sowing	Sds/cell
B	1	Leeks	Hannibal	01-Mar	2
B	1	Leeks	Bluegr. Winter	01-Mar	2
B	1	Leeks	Blue Solaise	20-May	2
B	2	Garlic	various	20-Feb	
B	2	Garlic	various	15-Oct	
B	3	Onion	Sturon	20-Mar	
B	4	Shallots	Zebrune	20-Feb	4
B	4	Shallots	various	10-Mar	
B	5	Scallions	Ishikura	01-Apr	10
B	5	Scallions	Ishikura	15-May	10
B	5	Scallions	Ishikura	01-Jul	10
B	6	Lettuce	various	01-Apr	3
B	6	Lettuce	various	01-May	3
B	6	Lettuce	various	01-Jun	3
B	6	Lettuce	various	01-Jul	3
B	6	Lettuce	various	01-Aug	3
C	1	Potato	Orla	15-Mar	
C	2	Potato	Sarpo Mira	15-Apr	
C	3	Potato	Vitabella	15-Apr	
C	4	Potato	Sevilla	15-Apr	

Qty	Planting	Harvest	Clearing	Area	Spacing cm
36 pl	15-Apr	Aug	Oct	2m	15 x 45
36 pl	15-Apr	Oct	Feb	2m	15 x 45
36 pl	05-Jul	March	May	2m	15 x 45
48 pl	direct	Aug	Aug	3m	25 x 25
48 pl	direct	July	Aug	3m	25 x 25
320 sets	direct	July	Aug	8m	10 x 25
72 pl	01-Apr	July	Aug	2m	30 x 30
18 sets	direct	July	Aug	2m	30 x 30
8 bun	01-May	June	July	0.5m	25 x 25
8 bun	15-Jun	July	Aug	0.5m	25 x 25
8 bun	01-Aug	Sep	Oct	0.5m	25 x 25
16 pl	01-May	June	July	1m	25 x 25
16 pl	01-Jun	July	Aug	1m	25 x 25
16 pl	01-Jul	Aug	Sep	1m	25 x 25
16 pl	01-Aug	Sep	Oct	1m	25 x 25
16 pl	01-Sep	Oct	Nov	1m	25 x 25
64 tub	direct	July	Sep	6m	25 x 75
48 tub	direct	Sep	Oct	6m	30 x 75
48 tub	direct	Sep	Oct	6m	30 x 75
48 tub	direct	Sep	Oct	6m	30 x 75

Plot	Bed	Crop	Variety	Sowing	Sds/cell
C	5	Courgette	various	25-Apr	1
C	5	Squashes	various	01-May	1
C	6	Pumpkins	various	01-May	1
D	1	Carrots	Romance F1	31-May	
D	2	Celeriac	Giant Prague	20-Mar	1
D	2	Celery	Victoria F1	10-Apr	1
D	3	Beetroot	Pablo F1	15-Apr	
D	3	Beetroot	Cylindra	20-May	
D	4	Parsnip	Javelin F1	01-May	
D	5	Carrots	Romance F1	15-Apr	
D	5	Spin P & Chard	various	01-Apr	1
D	6	Beetroot	Pablo F1	20-May	
D	6	Spin P & Chard	various	25-May	1
E	1	Beans, Broad	Witkeim	01-Mar	
E	1	Beans, Broad	Aquad. Claudia	15-Oct	
E	2	Beans, Runner	Enorma	20-May	
E	2	Pea	all types	15-Apr	
E	3	Beans, Cl. Fr.	Cobra	20-May	

Qty	Planting	Harvest	Clearing	Area	Spacing cm
3 pl	30-May	July	Oct	3m	90 x 90
5 pl	01-Jun	Sep	Oct	6m	2m
5 pl	01-Jun	Sep	Oct	3m	2m
2 packs	direct	Oct	Oct	6m	4 x 25
45 pl	20-May	Sep	Oct	5m	35 x 35
12 pl	10-Jun	Aug	Sep	1m	27 x 27
1 pack	direct	July	Sep	3m	10 x 25
1 pack	direct	Oct	Oct	3m	10 x 25
2 packs	direct	Oct	Jan	6m	10 x 25
2 packs	direct	July	Sep	3m	4 x 25
18 pl	01-May	July	Sep	2m	35 x 35
1 pack	direct	Oct	Oct	4m	10 x 25
18 pl	25-Jun	Aug	Nov	2m	35 x 35
90 sds	direct	July	Aug	4m	15 x 45
45 sds	direct	June	July	2m	15 x 45
1 pack	direct	Aug	Oct	2m	4pl/30cm
160	direct	July	Aug	4m	5cm
1 pack	direct	Aug	Oct	1m	4pl/30cm

NOTES

Polytunnel for the self-sufficient garden

A polytunnel is essential for a self-sufficient garden. You can extend the growing season for most crops, as well as growing warmth loving crops which can't be grown in our climate.

The tunnel size I would suggest for the complete self-sufficient garden measures 8m x 12m (92m²). There are many suppliers around and I suggest you compare a few prices before buying a tunnel. If you were to grow and sell high-value crops from your tunnel, you will be able to recoup the cost of the tunnel in one year.

If you are considering expanding in the future, I would recommend a commercial tunnel measuring 9m x 20m (180m²). Even if it is not fully used in the first couple of years you will get an additional weather-proof outdoor space. I even saw one tunnel with a swimming pool in it!

Greenhouses are generally better for plants and also nicer to look at but, unfortunately are also a lot more expensive.

In the following pages you'll find a drawing of the beds and a table with all the crops and their sowing dates.

I do all my planning on an excel spreadsheet. Once it is set up, all future planning is far easier.

For more detailed information on tunnel management and growing techniques for each crop, refer to my my previous book: "Fruit & Vegetables for the Polytunnel and Greenhouse".

Tunnel - Winter/Spring

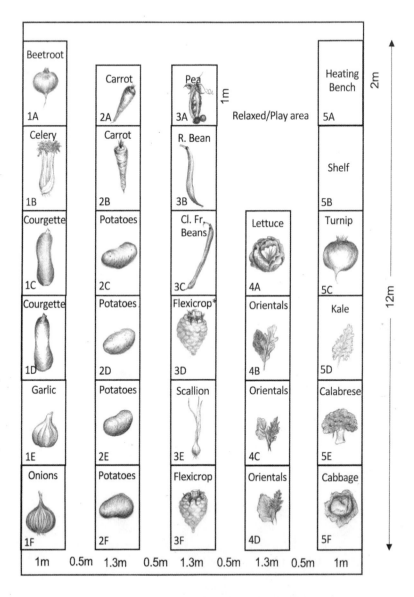

Beetroot **1A**	Carrot **2A**	Pea **3A**	Relaxed/Play area	Heating Bench **5A**
Celery **1B**	Carrot **2B**	R. Bean **3B**		Shelf **5B**
Courgette **1C**	Potatoes **2C**	Cl. Fr. Beans **3C**	Lettuce **4A**	Turnip **5C**
Courgette **1D**	Potatoes **2D**	Flexicrop* **3D**	Orientals **4B**	Kale **5D**
Garlic **1E**	Potatoes **2E**	Scallion **3E**	Orientals **4C**	Calabrese **5E**
Onions **1F**	Potatoes **2F**	Flexicrop **3F**	Orientals **4D**	Cabbage **5F**

1m   0.5m   1.3m   0.5m   1.3m   0.5m   1.3m   0.5m   1m

2m

12m

1m

Flexicrop is any crop you would like to grow more of.

Tunnel – Summer/Autumn

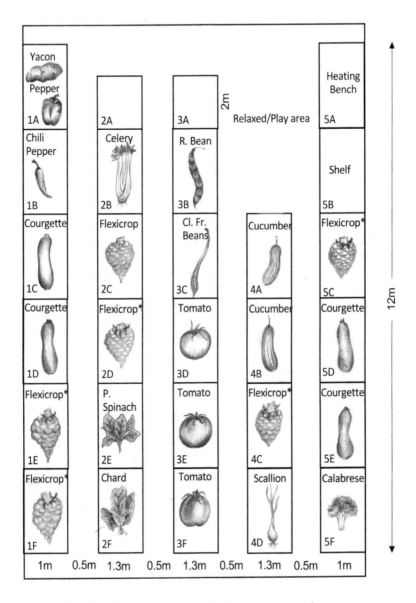

Yacon Pepper 1A	2A	3A	2m Relaxed/Play area	Heating Bench 5A
Chili Pepper 1B	Celery 2B	R. Bean 3B		Shelf 5B
Courgette 1C	Flexicrop 2C	Cl. Fr. Beans 3C	Cucumber 4A	Flexicrop* 5C
Courgette 1D	Flexicrop* 2D	Tomato 3D	Cucumber 4B	Courgette 5D
Flexicrop* 1E	P. Spinach 2E	Tomato 3E	Flexicrop* 4C	Courgette 5E
Flexicrop* 1F	Chard 2F	Tomato 3F	Scallion 4D	Calabrese 5F
1m	0.5m 1.3m	0.5m 1.3m	0.5m 1.3m 0.5m	1m

12m

Flexicrop is any crop you would like to grow more of.

Crop plan for polytunnel

Bed	Crop	Variety	Sowing	Sds/cell
1	Beetroot	Pablo F1	01-Feb	
1	Beetroot	Pablo F1	01-Mar	
1	Celery	Victoria F1	15-Feb	1
1	Celery	Victoria F1	31-Mar	1
1	Courgette	various	15-Mar	1
1	Courgette	various	15-Jun	1
1	Garlic	various	15-Oct	
1	Onion	Troy	15-Sep	
1	Pepper, Chilli	various	15-Feb	1
1	Pepper, sweet	various	15-Feb	1
1	Yacon	white	15-Mar	
2	Carrots	Amst. Forcing	31-Jan	
2	Carrots	Early Nantes	01-Mar	
2	Celery	Victoria F1	10-Jun	1
2	Potato	early	25-Jan	
2	Potato	Orla	01-Mar	
2	Spin P & Chard	various	31-Jan	1
3	Beans, Cl. Fr.	Cobra	15-Mar	
3	Beans, Cl. Fr	Borlotto	15-Apr	
3	Beans, Runner	Enorma	15-Mar	
3	Pea	all types	15-Feb	
3	Scallions	Ishikura	01-Feb	10
3	Scallions	Ishikura	01-Mar	10

Qty	Planting	Harvest	Clearing	Area	Spacing cm
1 pack	direct	May	June	1m	10 x 25
1 pack	direct	June	June	1m	10 x 25
12 pl	15-Apr	June	July	1m	27 x 27
12 pl	31-May	July	Aug	1m	27 x 27
3 pl	25-Apr	May	Aug	3m	90 x 90
3 pl	15-Jul	Sep	Nov	3m	90 x 90
16 pl	direct	May	June	1m	25 x 25
80	direct	May	May	2m	10 x 25
8 pl	15-May	July	Oct	2m	45 x 45
12	15-May	July	Sep	3m	45 x 45
1 pl	28-Apr	Oct	Nov	1m	1m
1 pack	direct	May	June	2m	4 x 25
1 pack	direct	June	June	2m	4 x 25
12 pl	10-Aug	Sep	Oct	1m	27 x 27
32 tub	direct	May	June	4m	25 x 40
32 tub	direct	June	June	4m	25 x 40
9 pl	01-Mar	April	June	1m	35 x 35
1 pack	direct	May	Aug	2m	4pl/30cm
1 pack	direct	Aug	Sep	2m	4pl/30cm
1 pack	direct	May	Aug	1m	4pl/30cm
80	direct	May	June	2m	5cm
8 bun	01-Mar	April	May	0.5m	25 x 25
8 bun	01-Apr	May	June	0.5m	25 x 25

Bed	Crop	Variety	Sowing	Sds/cell
3	Spin P & Chard	various	01-Sep	1
3	Tomato	various	20-Feb	1
4	Cucumber	Passandra F1	20-Apr	1
4	Cucumber	Passandra F1	15-Jun	1
4	Lettuce	various	01-Feb	3
4	Lettuce	various	01-Mar	3
4	Lettuce	various	01-Aug	3
4	Lettuce	various	01-Sep	3
4	Oriental Salads	various	01-Feb	5
4	Oriental Salads	various	01-Mar	5
4	Oriental Salads	various	15-Sep	5
4	Scallions	Ishikura	01-Aug	10
4	Scallions	Ishikura	01-Sep	10
5	Cabbage	Hispi F1	25-Jan	1
5	Cabbage	Hispi F1	25-Feb	1
5	Calabrese	Tiara F1	25-Jan	1
5	Calabrese	Tiara F1	01-Mar	1
5	Calabrese	Chevalier F1	10-Jul	1
5	Calabrese	Chevalier F1	10-Aug	1
5	Kale	various	25-Jan	1
5	Kale	various	01-Sep	1
5	Turnip	P Top Milan	31-Jan	1
5	Turnip	P Top Milan	01-Mar	1

Qty	Planting	Harvest	Clearing	Area	Spacing cm
27 pl	01-Oct	Nov	March	3m	35 x 35
20 pl	05-May	July	Oct	5m	50 x 50
2 pl	20-May	July	Sep	1m	50cm
4 pl	15-Jul	Aug	Oct	2m	50cm
16 pl	01-Mar	April	May	1m	25 x 25
16 pl	01-Apr	May	June	1m	25 x 25
16 pl	01-Sep	Oct	Nov	1m	25 x 25
16 pl	01-Oct	Nov	March	1m	25 x 25
16 pl	01-Mar	April	May	1m	20 x 25
16 pl	01-Apr	May	June	1m	20 x 25
48 pl	15-Oct	Nov	March	4m	20 x 25
8 bun	01-Sep	Oct	Oct	0.5m	25 x 25
8 bun	01-Oct	Oct	Nov	0.5m	25 x 25
12 pl	01-Mar	April	May	1m	25 x 25
12 pl	25-Mar	May	June	1m	25 x 25
6 pl	25-Feb	April	May	1m	45 x 45
6 pl	01-Apr	May	June	1m	45 x 45
6 pl	10-Aug	Oct	Oct	1m	45 x 45
6 pl	10-Sep	Nov	Nov	1m	45 x 45
9 pl	25-Feb	April	July	1m	30 x 30
9 pl	01-Oct	Jan	March	1m	30 x 30
24 pl	05-Feb	April	May	1m	15 x 25
24 pl	01-Apr	May	June	1m	15 x 25

Sowing plan for the complete self - sufficient garden

(includes the outdoor garden - G and polytunnel -P)

Area	Plot	Bed	Crop	Variety	Sowing	Sds/cell
P		2	Potato	early	25-Jan	
P		5	Cabbage	Hispi F1	25-Jan	1
P		5	Calabrese	Tiara F1	25-Jan	1
P		5	Kale	various	25-Jan	1
P		2	Carrots	Amst. Forcing	31-Jan	
P		2	Spin P & Chard	various	31-Jan	1
P		5	Turnip	Purple Top Milan	31-Jan	1
P		1	Beetroot	Pablo F1	01-Feb	
P		3	Scallions	Ishikura	01-Feb	10
P		4	Lettuce	various	01-Feb	3
P		4	Oriental Salads	various	01-Feb	5
P		1	Celery	Victoria F1	15-Feb	1
P		1	Pepper, Chilli	various	15-Feb	1
P		1	Pepper, sweet	various	15-Feb	1
P		3	Pea	all types	15-Feb	
G	B	2	Garlic	various	20-Feb	
G	B	4	Shallots	Zebrune	20-Feb	4
P		3	Tomato	various	20-Feb	1
P		5	Cabbage	Hispi F1	25-Feb	1
G	B	1	Leeks	Hannibal	01-Mar	2
G	B	1	Leeks	Bluegr. Winter	01-Mar	2
G	E	1	Beans, Broad	Witkeim	01-Mar	
P		1	Beetroot	Pablo F1	01-Mar	
P		2	Carrots	Early Nantes	01-Mar	

Qty	Planting	Harvest	Clearing	Area	Spacing cm
32 tub	direct	May	June	4m	25 x 40
12 pl	01-Mar	April	May	1m	25 x 25
6 pl	25-Feb	April	May	1m	45 x 45
9 pl	25-Feb	April	July	1m	30 x 30
1 pack	direct	May	June	2m	4 x 25
9 pl	01-Mar	April	June	1m	35 x 35
24 pl	05-Feb	April	May	1m	15 x 25
1 pack	direct	May	June	1m	10 x 25
8 bun	01-Mar	April	May	0.5m	25 x 25
16 pl	01-Mar	April	May	1m	25 x 25
16 pl	01-Mar	April	May	1m	20 x 25
12 pl	15-Apr	June	July	1m	27 x 27
8 pl	15-May	July	Oct	2m	45 x 45
12	15-May	July	Sep	3m	45 x 45
80	direct	May	June	2m	5cm
48 pl	direct	Aug	Aug	3m	25 x 25
72 pl	01-Apr	July	Aug	2m	30 x 30
20 pl	05-May	July	Oct	5m	50 x 50
12 pl	25-Mar	May	June	1m	25 x 25
36 pl	15-Apr	Aug	Oct	2m	15 x 45
36 pl	15-Apr	Oct	Feb	2m	15 x 45
90 seeds	direct	July	Aug	4m	15 x 45
1 pack	direct	June	June	1m	10 x 25
1 pack	direct	June	June	2m	4 x 25

Area	Plot	Bed	Crop	Variety	Sowing	Sds/cell
P		2	Potato	Orla	01-Mar	
P		3	Scallions	Ishikura	01-Mar	10
P		4	Lettuce	various	01-Mar	3
P		4	Oriental Salads	various	01-Mar	5
P		5	Calabrese	Tiara F1	01-Mar	1
P		5	Turnip	Purple Top Milan	01-Mar	1
G	B	4	Shallots	various	10-Mar	
G	G	3	Artichoke, Jer	various	10-Mar	
G	C	1	Potato	Orla	15-Mar	
G		2	Yacon	white & purple	15-Mar	
P		1	Courgette	various	15-Mar	1
P		1	Yacon	white	15-Mar	
P		3	Beans, Cl. Fr.	Cobra	15-Mar	
P		3	Beans, Runner	Enorma	15-Mar	
G	A	4	Calabrese	Chevalier F1	20-Mar	1
G	B	3	Onion	Sturon	20-Mar	
G	D	2	Celeriac	Giant Prague	20-Mar	1
P		1	Celery	Victoria F1	31-Mar	1
G	A	3	Cabbage	Stonehead F1	01-Apr	1
G	B	5	Scallions	Ishikura	01-Apr	10
G	B	6	Lettuce	various	01-Apr	3
G	D	5	Spin P & Chard	various	01-Apr	1
G	A	1	Kale	various	05-Apr	1
G	D	2	Celery	Victoria F1	10-Apr	1
G	A	6	Turnip/Swede	mixed	15-Apr	1
G	C	2	Potato	Sarpo Mira	15-Apr	
G	C	3	Potato	Vitabella	15-Apr	

Qty	Planting	Harvest	Clearing	Area	Spacing cm
32 tub	direct	June	June	4m	25 x 40
8 bun	01-Apr	May	June	0.5m	25 x 25
16 pl	01-Apr	May	June	1m	25 x 25
16 pl	01-Apr	May	June	1m	20 x 25
6 pl	01-Apr	May	June	1m	45 x 45
24 pl	01-Apr	May	June	1m	15 x 25
18 sets	direct	July	Aug	2m	30 x 30
20 tub	direct	Nov	Feb	6m	30 x 90
64 tub	direct	July	Sep	6m	25 x 75
2 pl	31-May	Oct	Nov	2m	1m
3 pl	25-Apr	May	Aug	3m	90 x 90
1 pl	28-Apr	Oct	Nov	1m	1m
1 pack	direct	May	Aug	2m	4pl/30cm
1 pack	direct	May	Aug	1m	4pl/30cm
6 pl	20-Apr	June	July	1m	45 x 45
320 sets	direct	July	Aug	8m	10 x 25
45 pl	20-May	Sep	Oct	5m	35 x 35
12 pl	31-May	July	Aug	1m	27 x 27
12 pl	01-May	July	Sep	2m	40 x 40
8 bun	01-May	June	July	0.5m	25 x 25
16 pl	01-May	June	July	1m	25 x 25
18 pl	01-May	July	Sep	3m	35 x 35
6 pl	05-May	July	Sep	1m	45 x 45
12 pl	10-Jun	Aug	Sep	1m	27 x 27
72 pl	15-May	July	Sep	3m	15 x 25
48 tub	direct	Sep	Oct	6m	30 x 75
48 tub	direct	Sep	Oct	6m	30 x 75

Area	Plot	Bed	Crop	Variety	Sowing	Sds/cell
G	C	4	Potato	Sevilla	15-Apr	
G	D	3	Beetroot	Pablo F1	15-Apr	
G	D	5	Carrots	Romance F1	15-Apr	
G	E	2	Pea	all types	15-Apr	
P		3	Beans, Cl. Fr	Borlotto	15-Apr	
G	A	4	Calabrese	Chevalier F1	20-Apr	1
P		4	Cucumber	Passandra F1	20-Apr	1
G	A	2	Br sprouts	Brigitte F1	24-Apr	1
G	A	3	Cabbage	Rodynda	25-Apr	1
G	C	5	Courgette	various	25-Apr	1
G	A	1	Kale	various	28-Apr	1
G	B	6	Lettuce	various	01-May	3
G	C	5	Squashes	various	01-May	1
G	C	6	Pumpkins	various	01-May	1
G	D	4	Parsnip	Javelin F1	01-May	
G	B	5	Scallions	Ishikura	15-May	10
G	A	3	Cabbage	January King	20-May	1
G	A	4	Cabbage	Vertus	20-May	1
G	A	4	Calabrese	Chevalier F1	20-May	1
G	B	1	Leeks	Blue Solaise	20-May	2
G	D	3	Beetroot	Cylindra	20-May	
G	D	6	Beetroot	Pablo F1	20-May	
G	E	2	Beans, Runner	Enorma	20-May	
G	E	3	Beans, Cl. Fr.	Cobra	20-May	
G	A	5	Swede	Gowrie	25-May	1
G	D	6	Spin P & Chard	various	25-May	1

Qty	Planting	Harvest	Clearing	Area	Spacing cm
48 tub	direct	Sep	Oct	6m	30 x 75
1 pack	direct	July	Sep	3m	10 x 25
2 packs	direct	July	Sep	3m	4 x 25
160	direct	July	Aug	4m	5cm
1 pack	direct	Aug	Sep	2m	4pl/30cm
6 pl	20-May	July	Aug	1m	45 x 45
2 pl	20-May	July	Sep	1m	50cm
1 pack	24-May	Oct	Dec	3m	90 x 90
12 pl	25-May	Sep	Nov	2m	45 x 45
3 pl	30-May	July	Oct	3m	90 x 90
6 pl	28-May	Aug	Nov	1m	45 x 45
16 pl	01-Jun	July	Aug	1m	25 x 25
5 pl	01-Jun	Sep	Oct	6m	2m
5 pl	01-Jun	Sep	Oct	3m	2m
2 packs	direct	Oct	Jan	6m	10 x 25
8 bun	15-Jun	July	Aug	0.5m	25 x 25
12 pl	20-Jun	Oct	Jan	2m	45 x 45
12 pl	20-Jun	Nov	Feb	2m	45 x 45
6 pl	20-Jun	Aug	Sep	1m	45 x 45
36 pl	05-Jul	March	May	2m	15 x 45
1 pack	direct	Oct	Oct	3m	10 x 25
1 pack	direct	Oct	Oct	4m	10 x 25
1 pack	direct	Aug	Oct	2m	4pl/30cm
1 pack	direct	Aug	Oct	1m	4pl/30cm
120pl	25-Jun	Oct	Nov	5m	20 x 30
18 pl	25-Jun	Aug	Nov	2m	35 x 35

Area	Plot	Bed	Crop	Variety	Sowing	Sds/cell
G	D	1	Carrots	Romance F1	31-May	
G	B	6	Lettuce	various	01-Jun	3
G	E	3	Pea	all types	01-Jun	
G	A	6	Kale	various	03-Jun	1
P		2	Celery	Victoria F1	10-Jun	1
G	A	2	Br sprouts	Brigitte F1	15-Jun	1
G	A	4	Calabrese	Chevalier F1	15-Jun	1
G	A	6	Oriental Salads	various	15-Jun	5
P		1	Courgette	various	15-Jun	1
P		4	Cucumber	Passandra F1	15-Jun	1
G	A	1	Broccoli, Spr.	mixed	25-Jun	1
G	B	5	Scallions	Ishikura	01-Jul	10
G	B	6	Lettuce	various	01-Jul	3
P		5	Calabrese	Chevalier F1	10-Jul	1
G	A	6	Oriental Salads	various	15-Jul	5
G	B	6	Lettuce	various	01-Aug	3
P		4	Lettuce	various	01-Aug	3
P		4	Scallions	Ishikura	01-Aug	10
P		5	Calabrese	Chevalier F1	10-Aug	1
G	A	6	Oriental Salads	various	15-Aug	5
P		3	Spin P & Chard	various	01-Sep	1
P		4	Lettuce	various	01-Sep	3
P		4	Scallions	Ishikura	01-Sep	10
P		5	Kale	various	01-Sep	1
P		1	Onion	Troy	15-Sep	
P		4	Oriental Salads	various	15-Sep	5
G	B	2	Garlic	various	15-Oct	
G	E	1	Beans, Broad	Aquad. Claudia	15-Oct	
P		1	Garlic	various	15-Oct	

Qty	Planting	Harvest	Clearing	Area	Spacing cm
2 packs	direct	Oct	Oct	7m	4 x 25
16 pl	01-Jul	Aug	Sep	1m	25 x 25
160	direct	Aug	Sep	4m	5cm
6 pl	03-Jul	Oct	Feb	1m	45 x 45
12 pl	10-Aug	Sep	Oct	1m	27 x 27
1 pack	15-Jul	Dec	Feb	3m	90 x 90
6 pl	15-Jun	Sep	Oct	1m	45 x 45
16 pl	15-Jul	Aug	Sep	1m	20 x 25
3 pl	15-Jul	Sep	Nov	3m	90 x 90
4 pl	15-Jul	Aug	Oct	2m	50cm
6 pl	25-Jul	Feb	May	4m	75 x 75
8 bun	01-Aug	Sep	Oct	0.5m	25 x 25
16 pl	01-Aug	Sep	Oct	1m	25 x 25
6 pl	10-Aug	Oct	Oct	1m	45 x 45
16 pl	15-Aug	Sep	Feb	1m	20 x 25
16 pl	01-Sep	Oct	Nov	1m	25 x 25
16 pl	01-Sep	Oct	Nov	1m	25 x 25
8 bun	01-Sep	Oct	Oct	0.5m	25 x 25
6 pl	10-Sep	Nov	Nov	1m	45 x 45
16 pl	15-Sep	Oct	Feb	1m	20 x 25
27 pl	01-Oct	Nov	March	3m	35 x 35
16 pl	01-Oct	Nov	March	1m	25 x 25
8 bun	01-Oct	Oct	Nov	0.5m	25 x 25
9 pl	01-Oct	Jan	March	1m	30 x 30
80 sets	direct	May	May	2m	10 x 25
48 pl	15-Oct	Nov	March	4m	20 x 25
48 pl	direct	July	Aug	3m	25 x 25
45 seeds	direct	June	July	2m	15 x 45
16 pl	direct	May	June	1m	25 x 25

Harvesting and storing

Artichoke, Jerusalem
Harvest the tubers from October onwards. They are best left in the ground over winter and harvested when required. If the garden is too wet in winter, the tubers should be harvested in late November and stored in boxes of damp soil.

Bean, broad
Harvest the beans when the pods are fully developed and the seeds are large enough but still tender. They should be picked on a weekly basis. If you have too many, they can be blanched and frozen. Pack in portion-sized freezer bags.

Bean, runner and French
Harvest the pods before they are full-sized, but still tender. If you have a glut, you can blanch and freeze the beans for use in winter. Pack them in family-sized freezer bags.

Beetroot
Summer beetroot can be harvested whenever you feel like it. The maincrop beetroot for storage should only be harvested in October. They can then be stored in boxes of sand or soil and will keep fresh until the following April. Beetroot can also be frozen, pickled or made into chutney.

Brussels sprouts
Harvest Brussels sprouts before the buds open. Always pick the lower sprouts first. Brussels sprouts can be blanched and frozen.

Calabrese
Harvest when the flower head is fully developed, but before the flowers begin to open. Cut 15cm below the flower head. After cutting the main head, the smaller side heads will develop. These should be cut on a regular basis. Calabrese can also be blanched and frozen.

Cabbage

Harvest when the heads are firm, but before they split open. Early varieties are more likely to split than winter ones. The flavour of savoy cabbages improves after frost and can be left outdoors. Dutch cabbages should be harvested in late October and stored in a cold, but frost-free, shed. I have become a great fan of sauerkraut in recent months – naturally given my heritage.

Carrot

Harvest the roots when they are about 3cm in diameter or smaller if you use the thinnings. If you want to store the carrots, leave them in the soil until October. Pull or dig them out carefully without damaging them and twist off the leaves. They can be stored in boxes of sand or soil until April. Young carrots can be blanched and frozen.

Celeriac

Harvest the roots as required from October until November. You can then lift the remaining crop, remove the leaves and store in boxes of damp sand or soil in a cool shed.

Celery

Harvest when the plants are about 30cm tall. Once they are ready, they may last about two to four weeks in the garden before becoming stringy. Once cut, they will last for about a week in a plastic bag in the fridge.

Chilli Pepper

Harvest chilli peppers throughout the summer. In late September, harvest the entire crop and dry.

Courgette

Start harvesting courgettes when the fruits are about 10cm long. Harvest at least twice per week. They are best if used fresh. Courgettes can be blanched and frozen.

Cucumber

I can't stress enough how important it is to harvest cucumbers regularly – at least every second day. Gluts of cucumbers can be pickled.

Garlic

Dig out carefully when leaves have turned yellow but before they fall over. Dry the bulbs thoroughly and store in a cool, dry place. Garlic can be used in pickles or for flavouring vinegars and oils.

Kale

Always harvest the lower leaves first. Harvest weekly and leave at least 7-8 leaves on the plant. Kale leaves keep for a week in a plastic bag in the fridge. There is little need to preserve kale as you can grow it all year round.

Leek

With the proper choice of varieties, you can harvest fresh leeks from July until March. Harvest as required as they don't store well. Before a cold spell you can dig out a dozen leeks, keep the roots on and store in a bucket with soil. Leeks can be blanched and frozen.

Lettuce

Start using lettuce as soon as the first hearts form. Once ready in the garden they will quickly bolt. Always grow small quantities at regular intervals to reduce wastage. If you harvest early in the morning, they will keep much better. If placed in a plastic bag in a fridge, they will keep for a week.

Onion

Harvest onions when most of the leaves have fallen. Loosen the roots with a fork and two weeks later pull out the onions and spread them out in the sun or in an open shed to let them dry. When completely dry, you can tie the onions in bunches with a string and store them in a cool, dry place.

Parsnip

Harvest the roots from mid-October onwards until early spring. Frost tends to improve the flavour. They can be left in the garden and used as required, or if your garden is too wet in winter, they can be stored in boxes of damp sand or soil in a cool shed or garage.

Pea, garden

Harvest when the pods are round and the seeds are fully formed but still tender. The seeds can be blanched and frozen.

Pea, sugar snap

Harvest when the pods are fully developed, but not yet stringy. Harvest and eat the entire pod. They can be blanched and frozen.

Pea, mangetout

Harvest when the pods are still flat and not stringy. If you have too many the excess can be blanched and frozen.

Potato

Harvest new potatoes as needed from July onwards. Only dig out what you need on a weekly basis as they continue to grow and don't store. Harvest maincrop potatoes in October and store in boxes of damp sand/soil or in a clamp. Only store healthy tubers.

Pumpkin

Harvest pumpkins for storage when the skins have hardened enough. Harvest before the first frost. They can be stored in a cool, frost-free shed for about three months. Leave the handles on the fruit otherwise they are more likely to rot.

Squash

Harvest summer squash when the fruit is young and tender. Winter squash should be harvested when mature, shortly before the last frost. They can be stored in a frost-free shed for 3 to 4 months depending on variety.

Swede

Harvest the roots when required from early autumn until spring. They can be left in the garden over winter or stored in boxes of sand or soil in a cool but frost-free shed.

Tomato

Harvest tomatoes when fully ripe. Do not leave ripe fruit on the vine.

Any excess fruit can be preserved in a variety of methods – freezing, ketchup, chutney, pickles and sauces.

Turnip

Harvest when roots are 5 to 10cm in diameter. They should be harvested regularly as older turnips become stringy. Young turnips can be blanched and frozen.

Storage of vegetables

Storing fresh vegetables:

Most fresh vegetables keep best in a plastic bag in the fridge. Remove the tops of root crops but do not wash. In the case of green vegetables (salads, spinach), they should be harvested early in the morning and immediately bagged and refrigerated.

Storing in the garden:

The following vegetables are frost-hardy and can be left in the soil throughout the winter and used as required up to early spring. It is beneficial to earth up exposed parts of the roots with soil or cover the beds with straw held down by netting. But, be aware that a straw covering may increase the slug damage to your crops.

However, outdoor storing is only recommended if your soil does not become waterlogged over winter. In this case, you may be better off storing them in boxes of damp sand or soil.

Examples include:
Carrot, celeriac, parsnip, swede, Jerusalem artichoke

Storing at room temperature:
The following vegetables can be stored at room temperature but out of direct sunlight:
Garlic, onion and shallots.

Storing loose in a cool but frost-free shed:
Some vegetables can be stored on wooden racks in a shed or garage or alternatively placed in net bags and hung up.

Examples include:
Dutch cabbage, squash, pumpkin

Storing in boxes of damp sand or soil (or a mixture) in a frost-free shed or garage:
This is by far the most reliable way of storing root vegetables over the winter months. In some years they will last until May the following year. Any container will do – wooden boxes, plastic bins or custom-built structures.

Alternate layers of damp sand/soil with vegetables. If the vegetables don't touch each other, diseases spread more slowly. A lid or wire netting is recommended to keep out potential vermin.

Some guidelines:
- Only store vegetables that have sufficiently matured in the garden. Mid-October is the best time to lift the crops.
- Never store damaged or diseased vegetables (eat them first!).
- Never wash root vegetables if you want to store them. It is sufficient to rub them clean. The surrounding soil layer protects the roots.
- Keep the sand/soil slightly moist.
- Check the contents monthly.

Examples include:
Beetroot, carrot, celeriac, parsnip, Jerusalem artichoke, potato and swede

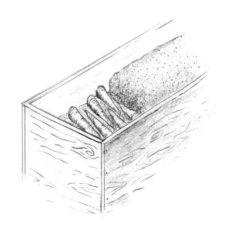

Storing in clamps:
This is the traditional storage method in Ireland. It is a useful way of storing your root crops over winter if you don't have space under cover. You do have to be aware of rodents, though. Clamps were traditionally placed outdoors but they work even better in a shed or barn.

How to make a clamp:
Place a free-draining material at the base of the pile (rushes or sand about 10 - 20cm depth). Stack your root crops in a pile on top of it with sloping sides, with the largest roots at the bottom. The width at the base should be around 60cm and the height of the finished clamp around 60cm high. Cover the pile with 20cm of rushes or straw and then with a 15cm layer of soil.
Examples include:
Potato, carrot, parsnip, celeriac, swede and beetroot

Potato Clamp

Freezing vegetables

In summer, you may often have gluts of vegetables and freezing is an easy way of preserving a wide range of vegetables. It's important to harvest them when they are at their best stage for eating and process them immediately. They should be prepared in the same way as you would use them for cooking.

Then they must be blanched before freezing. The word blanching may be confusing here as it also means, excluding the light through earthing up with soil or covering crops. Here, blanching refers to boiling vegetables for a short period of time before freezing. To blanch vegetables, you bring a large saucepan of lightly salted water to the boil, then put the prepared vegetables in a wire basket or large sieve and dip them into the boiling water for the recommended time period (see below).

Blanching times:
Bean, broad 3 mins
Bean, runner 2 mins
Brussels sprouts 4 mins
Peas 2 mins

You then lift out the wire basket and place it in a large bowl of cold water for a couple of minutes. Drain the vegetables and dry them on a towel.

You can then put the vegetables in freezer bags or boxes and remove as much air as possible by sucking the air out. It's advisable to label the bags with the name and the date. They should keep well for up to a year.

Other freezing methods

Beetroot
Use small beetroot, wash the roots and boil with the skin until tender. Rub off skin, cut in quarters, drain, cool, dry and freeze in rigid containers. They'll keep for 8 months.

Broccoli and calabrese
Divide into sprigs, blanch for 4 minutes, cool, drain and dry, then freeze in rigid containers and separate the layers with greaseproof paper. Cook frozen for 8 minutes.

Carrots
Wash, peel and dice carrots, blanch for 4 minutes, drain, cool, dry and freeze in a rigid container with 10mm space at the top.

Courgette
Trim off ends and cut into 2cm slices, blanch for 1 minute, drain, cool, dry and freeze in a rigid container with 10mm space at the top. They'll keep for 6 months, thaw them partially and fry in butter.

Leek
Remove the outer leaf and cut into 2cm slices, blanch for 2 minutes, drain, cool, dry and freeze in a rigid container with 10mm space at the top. They'll keep for 6 months, thaw them partially and fry in butter.

Parsnip
Wash, peel and cut parsnip into slices, blanch for 3 minutes, drain, cool, dry and freeze in a rigid container with 10mm space at the top.

Tomato
Tomatoes can be frozen whole. Remove the green stalk and place them in a single layer on a baking tray and freeze for 24 hours. Then transfer the frozen fruits into portion sized freezer bags.
They will only be suitable for cooking. If you have more time, cook a large batch tomato soup and freeze in small quantity.

Turnip
Wash, peel and cut turnips into 2cm slices, blanch for 2 minutes, drain, cool, dry and freeze in a rigid container with 10mm space at the top.

Sauerkraut

I make sauerkraut on a weekly basis and there is hardly a day I go without it. Home-made sauerkraut is infinitely better than any shop-bought product. It's completely different and shouldn't even be named the same. For some strange reason I have always thought it's too difficult to make and that it takes too long to mature. In fact, it's the opposite. It's so quick to make and it's ready within 5 to 7 days. Traditionally, it is left for months, but I prefer it crunchy with great texture which is at its best after 5 to 7 days.

All you need is cabbage and salt and a little spring water. Salting was a much more common method for preserving in the past.

Method:
1. Finely chop or shred a firm cabbage – I prefer red cabbage for it, but any cabbage would be suitable.
2. Place into a glazed earthenware or glass bowl and mix in the salt at a ratio of 1kg cabbage to 20g of coarse grained sea salt or Himalayan salt.
3. Massage the salt into the cabbage for 5 minutes.
4. Leave to stand for 1 hour and the salt will have started to draw out some juice from the cabbage.
5. Push/press the shredded cabbage into a large glass jar (preserving jar) with a wide neck. Keep compressing it with a spoon as you fill the jar. You'll be surprised how much you get into a jar.
6. When nearly full, weigh the cabbage down with a clean smaller jam jar, filled with stones. Cover with a clean tea towel.
7. Push in the cabbage down twice a day – you may need to add a very small quantity of spring water to submerge the cabbage.
8. The highly beneficial micro-organisms will do the work for you, both for the kraut and then for your stomach.

Pests, disease and weed prevention

Introduction

In an organic garden all emphasis should be placed on creating a healthy and resilient garden. There are very few control methods available and we don't really want to use them. This is why we chose to grow food organically – to avoid the use of chemicals in the garden and in our food. Within a couple of years you'll find that your garden has found its balance and then nature will sort out most problems.

In this book I'm not giving detailed descriptions of pests and diseases – please refer to the book, "Vegetables for the Irish Garden", which has an extensive chapter on this. Instead I focus on just the main points on how to create a healthy garden.

Right plant, right place, right time

Plants that are not suited to your climate and soil conditions will never thrive and, therefore will be the first ones to be attacked by pests and diseases. This seems nearly too obvious to state, but still it is the most common reason why plants fail. Choose the right types of crops for your location and use the correct sowing/planting date. For example, any butternut squash will struggle or fail in Ireland. You are better off planting a Crown Prince or Uchiki Kuri squash. Grow squashes in a sheltered part of the garden and only plant them outdoors in the first week of June (or last week in May with frost protection – fleece). If you want butternut squashes you need to grow them in a polytunnel. Right plant, right place, right time!

Healthy Soil

It's very simple, a healthy soil produces healthy plants and a poor soil produces poor plants which are prone to pests and diseases. The soil is the home of your plants. They are connected to the soil with their roots and spend all their life there.

Plants shouldn't be starving and they should also not be over-fed. As with people, if plants don't get enough 'food', they become weak and sick, but problems also occur if they get too much of some nutrients. This will cause soft lush growth which is much more appetising for many pests and diseases. This is especially the case with too much nitrogen.

The care of your soil is the most important duty of every gardener. It is the most effective method of preventing a pest or disease outbreak. The ideal soil is a loose, moist, humus rich soil full of worms and other soil life with a balanced nutrient content, including all the trace elements. It may take a good few years to achieve this, but even the poorest soil can be made very fertile again as long as we look after it and feed the myriad of life within the soil with composts, seaweed etc.

Biodiversity

A garden with good biodiversity is a lot less prone to sudden attacks of pests and diseases as there is a balance of pests and predators. To increase the biodiversity in your garden is probably one of the most rewarding pleasures in gardening. You have the opportunity to create habitats and homes for many living creatures that have been pushed to the edge mainly through the destruction of their habitats.

Beneficial habitats include:
- Pond
- Log or branch pile
- Dry stone wall or stone pile
- Native hedgerow and include fruiting shrubs
- Native trees
- Clump of nettles in the corner of your garden
- Wildflower patch

Design idea for a healthy garden

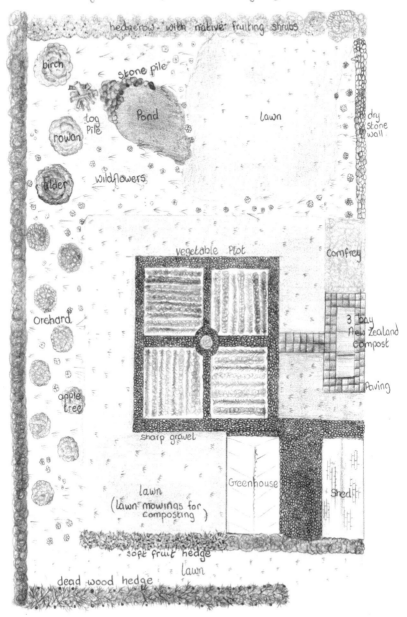

hedgerow with native fruiting shrubs

birch

stone pile

log pile

rowan

Pond

lawn

dry stone wall

alder

wildflowers

vegetable Plot

Comfrey

3 Bay New Zealand Compost

Paving

Orchard

sharp gravel

apple tree

lawn
(lawn mowings for composting)

Greenhouse

Shed

soft fruit hedge

lawn

dead wood hedge

Hygiene

Hygiene and order in and around the vegetable garden is very important for pest and disease prevention.

This seems contradictory to the previous chapter on biodiversity. Trust me on this – keep your vegetable plots neat and tidy. As you can see in the previous drawing, surround the vegetable patch ideally first with a gravel path and then a strip of lawn. The lawn should be mowed regularly and it'll make a good compost ingredient if mixed with a brown material such as leaves.

A vegetable garden within a wildflower area will most likely be gobbled up by slugs.

Your wildlife areas should be positioned a fair distance (minimum 5m) away from your plot as the beneficial creatures usually travel further and faster than the pests.

Resistant varieties

If you find that every year some of your crops get the same pests or diseases you should look out for resistant or tolerant varieties. There are now so many excellent new varieties of nearly all crops available with good resistance.

Examples:
Potato: Sarpo Mira, Seville, Carolus, Orla and Setanta are very resistant to potato blight
Pea: Hurst Greenshaft is very resistant to mildew
Parsnip: Gladiator F1 and Javelin F1 have some resistance to canker
Tomato: Mountain Magic F1 and Crimson Crunch F1 are resistant to blight
Tomato: Sungold F1 is resistant to greenback

The above are just a few examples and you'll find lots more when browsing through seed catalogues.

Timing of sowing

It is sometimes possible to avoid outbreaks of pests and diseases by adjusting the sowing or planting dates. The best example is to sow your carrots in late May or early June. This late sowing avoids the first generation of carrot root fly in May.

Adjusting the spacing

If plants are spaced too closely, they are a lot more susceptible to fungal diseases such as grey mould or mildew. If you want to lessen any potential problem, you can always space your crops a little bit further apart.

This increased airflow between the plants reduces the incidence of fungal diseases that thrive in more humid conditions.

Crop covers

Crop covers especially the bionet (also known as enviromesh) have become the saviours for many organic vegetable crops. These create barriers that keep flying or jumping pests away from your crops. In some gardens it is impossible to grow carrots without this special netting in place for the entire growing season.

Apart from the bionet, you can also get a horticultural fleece which is mainly used for frost protection but tends to rip if used outdoors and is better suited in a polytunnel. If birds are a problem, you can get a bird netting to keep them away.
The crop covers can be placed directly onto the crops and secured on the sides. Make sure there are no gaps anywhere. However, I prefer to have the crop covers on cloches. My favourite is a mobile cloche with bionet.

Make a wooden frame with 2 x 2" timber to fit your bed, drill parallel holes along the sides at a distance of 50cm apart exactly the width of strong rigid pipe, cut sections of the pipe to create the hoops and then cover securely with the bionet.

Collars

Collars are used around brassicas to prevent the cabbage root fly from laying its eggs near the cabbage stems. I'm not sure if it is totally effective but it's worth a try.

Traps

Beer traps to catch and kill slugs are often used by gardeners. Be careful though that you don't catch any ground beetles by mistake as they are the best slug predators in your garden. If you use this method, ensure that the lip of the container is above the soil surface to avoid beetles from drowning.
You can also buy yellow sticky tape from garden centres to catch flying pests such as aphids. They are very good as indicators to find out which pests you have, but they will not control pests sufficiently.

Handpicking

Handpicking larger pests such as slugs, caterpillars, leatherjackets or weevils can be quite efficient, especially in a small garden.

Biological control

Biological control includes attracting beneficial creatures that feed on pests as well as introducing predators by mail order. I'm very much in favour of the first method of creating a well-balanced garden. I only once purchased predators by mail. These were the Encarsia wasps for controlling the greenhouse whitefly on tomatoes, but this was many years ago.

The one that has become quite popular in recent years is called Nemaslug, which are nematodes that predate on slugs and snails. It appears to be quite effective for a number of months.

Examples of natural predators include:

Hoverflies - the larvae and adult hoverfly feed on aphids.
Lacewing – feed on aphids
Ladybirds – feed on aphids
Beetles – feed on slugs and many other small pests
Earwigs – most people believe they are pests but they also feed on aphids
Frogs – feed on slugs
Spiders – feed on aphids and flies

Sprays

I prefer not to use any sprays that kill the pests because they also kill their predators which were about to eat the pests. These include pyrethrum, derris, neem products, soft soap (insecticidal soap) and many more. Many of these are permitted in organic farming as they are fully biodegradable within 48 hours.

The only sprays I would use on a regular basis are plant tonics. I sometimes use compost teas, garlic and seaweed sprays. These strengthen the plants and possibly confuse the pests, but never kill them.

For grey mould on tomatoes I use a milk/water spray (1 part milk and 7 parts water) and spray it onto the affected part in three consecutive days.

Some copper products are permitted for blight control on potatoes. I prefer to use a blight resistant variety.

Common pests

Birds

Most birds are very beneficial to your garden as they consume many pests including slugs. But, sometimes they can also cause some damage. Early in spring, crows and other large birds may peck out your onion sets, pigeons may eat your young cabbage plants and most birds will love any fruit you grow. If you find that you have a recurring problem, simply put a bird net over the crops you want to protect.

Aphids

Aphids are one of the most common pests in any garden. There are many different species, often adapted to just one or two host plants. They feed by sucking the sap out of plants and thus, weakening them and making them more susceptible to fungal diseases. They also transmit viral diseases from one plant to another. Aphids are a lot more common in sheltered gardens. In exposed gardens they are often blown away from your vegetables. You can often trust natural predators to control them before too much damage is done.

Slugs and snails

Slugs and snails are possibly the most hated creatures in the garden and nearly every gardener has a nightmare tale about them.

However, slugs are an important part of the food chain – they help with decomposing organic materials and are an important food source for birds, beetles, hedgehogs and many other creatures. Slugs are only a problem if they are in the wrong place – in your vegetable garden. As you can see in the garden design illustration (p.99) the vegetable area is neat and tidy and surrounded by a gravel path and then a short lawn. Only outside of this area you'll find all the habitats for the predators – wildflower meadow, log pile, dry stone wall, pond etc.

In case there are still some slugs that stray into the vegetable garden, you can trap them by placing small pieces of timber (the size of this book) around newly planted vegetables. The wooden boards provide shelter for the slugs during the day and you can collect them first thing in the morning. You'll find that after a few weeks some ground beetles have moved in under the boards and do the collection for you.

Cabbage caterpillars

Caterpillars of the cabbage white butterfly are one of the biggest nuisance for anybody who tries to grow brassicas. Either protect the crop with a suitable crop cover, or handpick caterpillars on a regular basis.

Leatherjackets

Leatherjackets are the larvae of the crane fly ('daddy long legs'). They feed on the roots and stems of many different plants especially lettuce. There is no other organic control than to handpick the larvae. The only times you can find them is when you prepare your ground or after it has just nibbled through the stem of your newly planted lettuce.

As soon as you notice a small lettuce plant wilting, pull it out and carefully search the soil around and you will find the culprit. You can also try to trap them by placing a layer of grass clippings on the ground and cover this with thick cardboard or black plastic. After two days, you can check the trap and dispose of any larvae.

Cutworms

Cutworms are the caterpillars of various moth species. They feed on some root vegetables, brassicas and lettuce. As with leatherjackets, they often sever the stem at ground level and they can also be found near affected plants.

Wireworms

Wireworms are the larvae of the click beetle. They are thin, orange-brown larvae, about 2cm long with a hard body and three pairs of legs near the head. They kill seedlings by feeding on young stems and roots. They can also tunnel through potatoes and carrots. They are a problem in a new garden and after a few years they will decline. I've seen gardeners trapping them on halved potatoes placed below ground level. These traps need to be checked daily.

Common diseases

Plant diseases are a lot more difficult to identify than pests. Diseases are caused by fungi, bacteria and viruses and are very difficult to treat organically.

The best method to deal with diseases is to avoid them in the first place. If a plant becomes diseased there is often something wrong in the environment or in the soil.

A gardener should try to identify what caused the problem rather than reaching for a control that may create even more problems in the future.

Botrytis (grey mould)

This is one of the most common plant diseases which affects a wide range of plants. The symptoms are white-grey fungal growths on affected areas. It is difficult to control so keep your garden clean and remove any diseased leaves as soon as you notice them.

Mildew

Powdery and downy mildew are also common problems for many vegetables. Powdery mildew can be a serious problem on courgettes. Downy mildew is a serious problem for onions especially during wet summers.

Potato blight

The most effective method of preventing potato blight is to grow a resistant variety.

Alternatively, use a copper based spray, but be careful when using it and don't spray too much.

Weed control

There is no such thing as a weed – it's simply a plant growing in the wrong place – and who is to say? Many weeds are edible and also very nutritious (nettle, chickweed, ground elder, dandelion etc.) and have medicinal qualities.

The mineral content of the weeds is beneficial for the soil and weed compost also makes a brilliant soil improver. We should be more grateful to our weeds as valuable compost ingredients.

Weeds play an essential role in nature by covering bare soil as quickly as possible to protect the soil from erosion or leaching of nutrients. Weeds, however, do compete for nutrients, light, air and water with the crops you want to grow.

Weeds fall into three categories, annual, biennial and perennial weeds:
When you start your plot, you are likely to have more perennial weeds such as dandelions and docks. After a couple of years you should have the perennial weeds under control and then the annuals may have sneaked into your garden. They have adapted to the frequent cultivations in your vegetable plot. They are even dependent on you to prepare a nice seedbed for them.

Common annual weeds include chickweed, shepherd's purse, groundsel, hairy bittercress, fathen, speedwell and mayweed.

Biennial weeds complete their lifecycle from seed to seed in two years. These weeds have not really adapted themselves to vegetable garden conditions. As they require two years to mature any soil disturbance during this time will destroy them.

Perennial weeds last for more than two years. Many of them are extremely difficult to get rid of. They are great survivors. Their survival techniques include, underground storage organs from which they can regenerate if the plant is killed (lesser celandine), low lying rosettes which escape the mower (daisy, plantain), the capacity to regenerate from small root sections possibly from a rotavator or from digging (dock, dandelion).

Indicator plants

Wild plants can give you a good idea of how good your soil is, as they have adapted themselves to certain site and soil conditions. These are known as indicator plants.

Wild plants have the purpose of balancing and even improving soils. For example, thistles with their hollow stalks and roots, bring air into the soil; thus they improve compacted soils where they prefer to grow. Nettles prefer to grow in nutrient rich soils, especially near any kind of dumps and leave behind a very dark, fertile and humus rich soil. The coltsfoot with its large leaves grows well in wet, compacted soils. Its large leaves 'pump' water out of the ground.

Weeds – good or bad?

Weeds are only a problem if they grow close to your vegetables and compete for water, nutrients and light. This can cause a substantial loss in yield. Some vegetables with sparse foliage are more likely to be overrun with weeds. You will notice that your onions, carrots and leeks need a lot more weeding than crops with a better shading effect such as broad beans, cabbages and potatoes. Another problem with certain weeds is the fact they may harbour pests and diseases which may later spread on to your vegetable crops. Examples include, weeds in the brassica family such as shepherds purse which may spread various brassica pests and diseases. Weeds may also encourage fungal diseases by restricting the air-circulation around the vegetables.

Weeds make harvesting a lot more difficult, especially if you have prickly weeds like thistles and nettles. You also have to be careful when you grow oriental salad vegetables and use the cut-and-come-again technique for harvesting as some weeds may sneak into the plants and, while some of the weeds are edible (chickweed, hairy bittercress), others are poisonous (foxglove, groundsel, nightshade). Apart from all the real disadvantages, weeds also make your vegetable garden look less attractive.

Weeds are not always bad. They don't always compete with your vegetables and don't always harbour pests and diseases or encourage fungal diseases. Some of them are not invasive and taste quite nice in a salad. In fact, weeds have also some beneficial aspects: they protect bare soil and prevent erosion, they can provide a diverse microclimate and ecosystem as many of them may be food plants for other creatures. Their roots also help to improve the biological activity and structure of the soil.

Hoeing

Without weeds, you wouldn't have a reason to hoe and without hoeing you won't get a beautiful tilth through which water and air can penetrate easily. This tilth is just like our own skin and we surely do not want our pores clogged up!

When you hoe on a dry, sunny day you leave the weeds lying on the ground. This encourages the multitude of soil inhabitants to break them down and release the nutrients back to your crop.

Compost and manure management

Compost heaps and manure piles may be sources of weeds, both seeds and roots. If you manage to make a hot compost by frequent turning of the heap, you may possibly achieve a temperature of 60°C which is enough to kill most weed seeds and roots. This is, however, very rarely achieved on a small compost pile. So you should be careful what weeds you put in. If you weed before the plants flower there is obviously no danger.

While manure is an excellent organic fertiliser, you are often introducing new weeds (docks and rushes) into your garden. It is advisable to get a pile of manure at least three months before using it and turn it once or twice.

The use of transplants

If you raise your plants in modular trays they are between 4 to 6 weeks old before you plant them out into the garden. They are way ahead of the weeds. During this time you can use the stale seed bed technique.

Stale seed bed technique

Ideally, the seedbed should be prepared a few weeks before you intend to sow your crops. The ground preparation and repeated raking will stimulate new weeds to germinate. These can easily be controlled through raking or shallow hoeing in dry weather. The more often you do this, the more weeds can be controlled before you actually sow or plant a crop.

Growing under mulches

This method is frequently used by organic growers, especially for wider spaced crops, such as courgettes and pumpkins, but is also used for many other crops such as onion and garlic. There are various materials available:

Mypex (which lets air and water through, but not weeds)

Recycled paper mulches

Natural mulches (leafmould, green waste compost, composted bark, composted wood chippings, etc.)

Natural mulches also act as an excellent soil improver but, unfortunately, many of them also attract slugs. If you have a low slug population in your garden, it is well worth a try. The exception to this is well-matured and even, sieved compost.

Recommended tools

I honestly would be lost without two types of hoes – the oscillating hoe and the round hoe. The oscillating hoe is the easiest hoe to use. You simply swivel it along the ground. The round hoe (or draw hoe) is excellent to get weeds from underneath cabbage or lettuce leaves. For larger gardens, you can buy a wheel hoe, but it's only worth it if you cultivate at least half an acre. There are also various flame-weeders available, but they are rarely used in small vegetable gardens.

Practical tips:

-   Hoe on dry sunny days and hand weed when the ground is wet. When hoeing on a hot day the weeds can be just left on the ground to decompose.

-   Never hand weed where the hoe can reach, only hand weed around or between plants.

-   Hoe or weed when the plants are small as it is so much faster.

Seed saving

Saving your own seeds adds another useful dimension to a self-sufficient garden. For some crops, it is quite easy to save seeds while others are more complex and getting the seeds to fully mature and dry may be a challenge. However, when it works you'll be surprised by the generosity of nature.

One parsnip plant can yield enough seeds for the next 10 years – except they only keep for one year. Here are some pointers and simple guidelines on how to save seeds:

F1 Hybrids

An F_1 hybrid is simply the first cross between two parent varieties of a vegetable. For example, if you have two varieties of carrots flowering at the same time they will cross pollinate and produce an F_1 hybrid. Many gardeners are concerned about using F_1 hybrids and think they are genetically engineered, but it is quite a natural process that happens constantly in nature.

There is also the misconception that seeds from F_1 hybrids are infertile. This is also untrue, but they will not come true to type. That means they won't be the same as the F_1 hybrid. They become F_2 hybrids.

F_1 hybrids are always uniform and more vigorous. An F_2 hybrid becomes more variable. Most varieties have been developed through initial hybridisation. About 25 years ago, my mother started saving seeds from an F1 hybrid tomato and she kept selecting for the traits she liked. After about 6-12 years, this variety has become true to type and now it is a standard variety. This means we can save seeds from it and it will be the same again as the mother plant. I called this tomato after her – Iris. It produces the most delicious large, but smooth beef tomatoes (I'm biased of course).

One of the concerns is that if we stop using open-pollinated (or standard) varieties that they will become extinct.

To conclude, if you save seeds from an F_1 hybrid you can't expect to get the same offspring.

Botanical classification - genus and species

Each vegetable crop is grouped according to its botanical family, genus and species. For seed savers this is very important to remember. Different varieties of vegetables from the same species will cross-pollinate with each other, however, crosses between vegetables from different species are very rare.

To translate this:
Carrot – Apiaceae (family), *Daucus* (genus), *carota* (species). That means that all carrot varieties can cross-pollinate and also with the wild carrot which is also *Daucus carota*.

Courgette – Cucurbitaceae (family), *Cucurbita* (genus), *pepo* (species).

Courgettes will cross-pollinate with any other *Cucurbita pepo* type – For example Spaghetti squash, Connecticut pumpkin and Patty Pan squash.

Now it gets even more confusing – the Brassicas!

Cabbage, cauliflower, broccoli, Brussels sprouts, kale and kohlrabi are all *Brassica oleracea* and will easily cross-pollinate with each other. So if you want to save seeds that come true to type, you can only produce one type per year. Alternatively, you need to isolate them and grow them far apart. There are excellent books available – "Seed to Seed" by Suzanne Ashworth or "Breed your own Vegetable Varieties" by Carol Deppe.

If you want to create something new and unusual, let a few different *Brassica oleracea* flower and you will most certainly get some surprises. The newest vegetable on the market is the Flower Sprout or Kalettes – a cross between Brussels sprouts and kale. It grows like a Brussels sprout, but the buds are open like mini kale florets.

Annual or biennial

Many vegetables are biennials, they produce the vegetative parts and storage organs in the first year. In the second year they will flower and produce seeds.

Biennial vegetables crops include carrots, beetroot, parsnip, chard, perpetual spinach and celeriac and others.

Annual vegetables will produce seeds in the first year. These include tomatoes, peppers, chillies, lettuce, peas, beans etc.

Bolted plants

Sometimes plants bolt and run to seed prematurely – please do not save seeds from these plants as you would select for early bolting. Always select for good traits.

Self-pollinated plants

These contain both male and female flower parts within the same flower. Tomatoes and lettuce are self-pollinating. This allows you to grow a number of different varieties on the same land and still save seeds.

How to make a seed saver garden?

In October, select three of your best roots of the following vegetables: carrot, beetroot and parsnip and store them safely in a bucket of damp sand/soil in a cool but frost-free shed. Select the three best onion bulbs and store. Mark your three best winter leeks with bamboo canes and don't harvest.

In February the following year, plant all the root vegetables in groups of three per type about 45cm apart (you'll need 1m² per vegetable type). Plant the roots with their tips just below ground level, plant onions half-way into the soil and transplant leeks with plenty of soil still attached to the roots.

Plants will soon start to grow and you will need to give them strong support as some of them will grow well over 1m tall. They will start to flower in June, keep an eye out for ripe seeds. Take seed-heads off the plant when they are mature but before they fall. If they don't ripen fully, you can pull the whole plant out in autumn and hang it upside down in a dry shed over a sheet or in large paper bags.

It's advisable to do a germination test to make sure you'll get a good crop the following year. With peas and beans, you will need to leave a section of your crop completely unharvested – around 1m². Collect the seeds when the pods are brown and when the seeds rattle inside.

Tools

My recommendation is to buy only a few, but high-quality tools. Unfortunately, there are many useless tools for sale in many outlets. Good quality tools make gardening a lot easier and more pleasant.

Good tools are a rarity nowadays, but there are still some excellent suppliers and garden centres that stock them.

These are a great investment. It is far better to start off with the few essential ones and to buy the best, rather than to buy a whole set of an inferior quality. For starting a small vegetable plot there is no need to buy a large range of fancy gardening tools. I have never been a fan of powered tools, especially a rotavator, but if wisely used, it could save time in the completely self-sufficient garden.

The following tools are sufficient.

Spade – A spade is necessary for digging and edging. Get one with a stainless steel blade and wooden handle with a comfortable grip and correct length to suit your body.

Digging fork – These have straight, strong prongs used for digging or loosening the soil. I often prefer to dig with a fork rather than a spade. It seems gentler on the worms.

Manure fork – In Leitrim they call it a "Grape". It has four curved prongs, ideal for composting work and gentle digging on stone-free soil.

Rake – Try and find a good, strong, metal rake with a long, wooden handle. It's one of the most important gardening tools (after the hoe).

If I waste any time in the garden, it's by raking – trying to level the soil to create a fine tilth for sowing and planting.

Hoes - Hoeing is probably one of the most important gardening activities. I recommend two hoes, the oscillating hoe (175mm) and the onion hoe, also known as a round hoe. If you can afford a third type I recommend a ridging hoe – ideal for heavy work and earthing up potatoes and other crops.

Shovel – A shovel is required for many gardening jobs, especially for moving finished compost or gravel and other materials

Broadfork (Biofork) – This is optional, but what a wonderful tool. It may only be required for the larger completely self-sufficient garden. It loosens the soil, breaks compaction and you don't need to dig. It's a very effective tool.

Wheelbarrow – Try and get a good quality wheelbarrow with a good wheel, ideally a rubber wheel. A wheelbarrow is essential for the self-sufficient garden.

Hand trowel and hand fork – These are used for planting, weeding, ruffling the soil between plants – endless uses.

Secateurs – There are so many useless secateurs around, that either break or don't cut anything. I recommend the Swiss-made, Felco secateurs. They are expensive, but will last a lifetime.

Garden line – You can simply get some bailer twine and strong sticks or why not treat yourself to a custom-made garden line.

Measuring rod – A piece of timber, 2m long (5cm x 2.5cm) and mark it into useful measurements (20, 30, 40cm). This is ideal for measuring planting distances.

Watering cans – You'll need one watering can with a fine rose for seedlings in trays and one for watering crops.

Hosepipe and barrel – It's important to have easy access to water – you may even look into a rainwater collection system.

Tool care and maintenance

It is very good practice to wash your tools after use and store them in a dry shed. The handles should be oiled with boiled linseed oil once or twice a year.

Checklist of other items you'll need:

Seeds

Onion sets, garlic bulbs and seed potatoes

Seed compost (KKS peat free modular compost – approved organically)

Potting compost (KKS peat free potting compost – approved organically)

Pots – a range of different sizes – 7cm, 9cm and 12cm

Modular trays – my favourite type is the 77 cell Quickpots modular trays

Propagation and potting area

Heating bench

Hardening off area

A trailer load of old/ancient manure or compost

Bamboo canes or hazel rods – for pea and bean supports outdoors

Crop cover (fleece for frost protection in tunnel and bionet for pest protection outdoors)

Hand sprayer – for foliar feeds (e.g. garlic and seaweed)

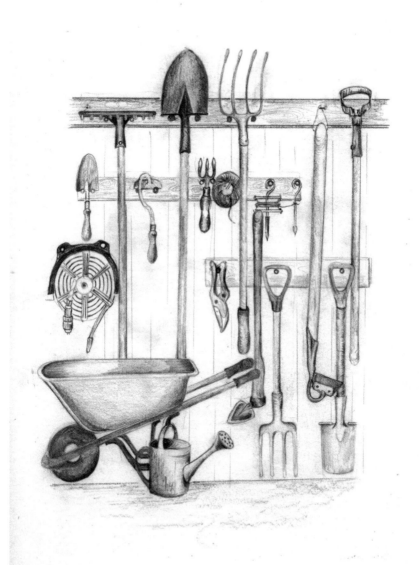

Vegetables A-Z

Artichoke, Jerusalem

Helianthus tuberosus

It's great to start the self-sufficiency book with my favourite vegetable – the one with the most potential, highest yield and certainly the easiest one you could grow. I have spent a number of years studying and growing this amazing crop and I'm in slight danger of filling the entire book with it.

Jerusalem artichokes are grown for their delicious and healthy tubers, similar in appearance to a knobbly potato. They are also grown just like potatoes, but expect them to reach 2-3m in height. The foliage looks like sunflowers and some varieties also flower profusely and produce numerous small "sunflowers".

The flavour of Jerusalem artichokes is not always agreeable to everyone at first and it may cause some unpleasant side effects after the first meal. Please stick to it – start with eating one tuber first and then increase the intake. It is one of the best sources of inulin, a resistant fiber that encourages all the good bacteria in our guts. You'll feel and even hear them mingling after a meal. Some people have nicknamed the poor Jerusalem artichoke 'fartichoke'!

Jerusalem artichokes are best grown on the same patch of land for many years. As they are very strong plants, any remaining tuber left in the ground after harvesting would become a weed for a follow-on crop.

Soil and site

Jerusalem artichokes can thrive in almost any soil but, the more fertile the soil, the higher the yield. They can also be grown as a windbreak.

In very exposed sites you could put fence posts at either end of the row and a plain wire across it to support them.

Plant Jerusalem artichokes on the north side of your vegetable plot so they won't shade your other crops.

Planting

Always select the best and least knobbly tubers to plant. You only ever need to buy tubers once! The tubers can be planted from late February to late March, as soon as the soil isn't too sticky. The plants are completely frost hardy.

Spacing

Jerusalem artichokes are best grown in drills like potatoes. If you have more than one drill, space the drills 90cm apart (from centre to centre). Plant the tubers 30cm apart in the drill and about 15cm deep. They benefit from being earthed up like potatoes.

Alternatively, they can be planted in a raised bed in a double or triple row and aim for a spacing of 45cm each way. You can earth them up by adding 5 to 10 cm of compost around the plants in May or June when the stalks are around 1m tall.

Ideally plant with the growth point up but it really does not matter, as they will grow even if you plant them upside down.

Rotation

Grow Jerusalem artichokes in the same bed every year. They have no specific pest or disease problems.

Harvesting and storing

You can start digging out tubers from November right through the winter. Alternatively, you can dig out the whole crop and store the tubers in boxes of moist sand/soil mixture. The tubers will keep until the following March/April.

Self-sufficiency – How much to grow?

Jerusalem artichokes are by far the most productive crop in terms of yield and nutrient value, yielding twice as much as potatoes and three times as much as carrots. Add to this the ease of growing and reliability compared to many other crops – it really deserves a prime permanent place in any garden.

Even if you are not too fond of them (yet), plant a bed of the flowering types at the back of your vegetable garden.

A 6m long drill can produce 60kg of Jerusalem artichoke tubers in good soil (or 40kg in average soil). You'll need to plant 3 tubers per meter – a total of 18 tubers.

Season: November – mid-February or 20 weeks.

<u>Summary</u>
A total of 6m² produces 40kg of tubers or 2kg per week for 20 weeks.

Potential problems
The only problem you may have is slugs eating the emerging shoots as they appear in early April. Keep a look out for signs about 3-4 weeks after planting and you may need some organic slug pellets at that time.

Varieties
Butler Berta
Chipolata
Earthing White
Fuseau
Gigante
Gotlanst Lilafleckig
Dwarf Sunray
Patata
Red Flame

Beans, Broad

Vicia faba

Introduction

Broad beans are an excellent source of protein for the self-sufficient garden. They are easy to grow, hardy and high yielding. If you love eating broad beans you need to grow them as they are often difficult to buy in shops. You can easily blanch and freeze them to get a year-round supply of beans.

Soil and site

Broad beans prefer to grow on an open site, as a result aphid infestation is minimised. Aphids spread rapidly in sheltered places. The soil should be well dug and reasonably fertile. Feed with compost rather than manure as too much nitrogen will inhibit nitrogen fixation from the air through rhizobium bacteria.

Sowing

Autumn types:
Sow directly 5cm deep in drills outdoors from early October until early November.

Spring types:
Sow directly 5cm deep in drills outdoors from late February until late April.

Some gardeners raise plants indoors for planting out and also sometimes grow the entire crop in a polytunnel – this is possible but for me, broad beans are a lazy no fuss crop and I sow seeds directly into the ground.

Spacing

Between plants: 15cm
Between rows: 45cm

Variety	Sowing	Location	Harvest	Area	Quantity
Aquadulce Claudia	15. Oct	Outdoors	May - Jun	2m²	45 seeds
Witkeim	1. Mar	Outdoors	July - Sep	4m²	90 seeds

Rotation

Broad beans should be rotated around the garden so that follow-on crops will benefit from nitrogen fixation.

Plant care

In exposed gardens broad beans may need some plant supports. A simple frame with bamboo canes is sufficient to prevent the plants from falling over. There are many years though when I don't support the plants and mostly they are strong enough to stand up against the wind.

Harvesting

Overwintered crops may be ready for harvesting from May onwards. Early spring sown beans will be cropping from June until August. Harvest the pods as soon as the seeds are fully formed but before they become too hard and mealy. Pick beans from the bottom upwards. Once the plants start to produce, harvest regularly at least once per week. Young small pods (2.5cm) can also be picked and eaten whole.

Storing

The seeds of broad bean can be blanched and deep-frozen and also dried.

Self-sufficiency - How much to grow?

Broad beans take up a lot of space, but are very important due to their nitrogen fixing capacity and by providing high protein food. A good plant for the soil, the garden and your health!

Autumn sown crop:
At a spacing of 15cm apart in the row and 3 rows per bed you'll need to sow 21 seeds per m². One square metre of broad beans will yield about 4kg of beans leaving about 1kg of shelled beans. Thus, 2m² sown in October will produce 2kg of actual beans from June to July.

Spring sown crop:
At a spacing of 15cm apart in the row and 3 rows per bed you'll need to sow 21 seeds per m². One square metre of broad beans will yield about 4kg of beans leaving about 1kg of shelled beans. Thus, 4m² sown in October will produce 4kg of actual beans from July to August.

Summary
A total of 6m² produces 6kg of beans (actual beans). If you blanch and freeze them in 150g bags – you'll get a 40 weeks supply of broad beans.

Potential problems

Black bean aphid (commonly known as blackfly) is the most common pest, attacking mainly the new soft growth at the top of the plant, especially in summer. When plants are fully grown, the tops can be nipped out.
The pea and bean weevils will notch the leaves of broad beans but this has very little effect on the yield, so no treatment is necessary.

Chocolate spot is characterised by small brown spots on the leaves, stems and pods. This disease will appear every year – early planting is essential so that the plant has matured before the disease appears.

Varieties

Autumn types:
Aquadulce Claudia
Super Aquadulce

Spring types:
Witkeim – this is by far the best with strong sturdy growth and a high yield of delicious beans, in fact it is so good that I wouldn't grow any other variety.

Beans, Climbing French & Runner

Phaseolus vulgaris
Phaseolus coccineus

Introduction

French and runner beans are a great source of home-grown, delicious, protein food. There are climbing and bushy types. The whole pods can be eaten when immature. I group them here together as the growing requirements are quite similar. There is great variation in pod types in French beans: green, yellow, purple or speckled. They may be flat, round, pencil shaped, long or short. The dwarf French beans grow to about 40cm high with a 25-30cm spread. Climbing types may grow over 2.4m high. Runner bean pods are generally flat and longer with a slightly downy, hairy skin.

For self-sufficiency, and to get most out of your garden I would recommend growing the Climbing French bean variety 'Cobra' – for many years my one and only! It produces a high yield of long, smooth, oval-shaped pods – rarely matched by any other one. In my opinion, the best runner bean variety is 'Enorma'.

Especially for the self-sufficient garden, you can grow an Italian dry bean variety such as "Borlotto Lingua di Fuoco". The dried seeds keep for a long time.

Soil and site

French and runner beans require a very sunny and sheltered site. The soil should be fertile, moisture-retentive and free-draining.
If you do not have a sheltered garden or live in a cooler part of the country you should grow climbing French beans in the polytunnel or greenhouse. Runner beans are slightly hardier than climbing French beans.

Sowing

Sow 5 seeds into 9cm pots about 4-5cm deep and plant out 4 weeks later. Alternatively, sow five seeds directly around each cane or string. The seeds need a minimum soil temperature of 12°C.

Type	Variety	Sow	Location	Harvest	Area	Qty
R. bean	Enorma	15. Mar	Polytunnel	Jun-Aug	1m²	30 sds
R. bean	Enorma	20. May	Outdoors	Aug-Oct	2m²	60 sds
Cl. Fr bean	Cobra	15. Mar	Polytunnel	May-Aug	1m²	30 sds
Cl. Fr Bean	Cobra	20. May	Outdoors	Aug-Oct	1m²	30 sds
Cl. Fr Bean	Borlotto	15. Apr	Polytunnel	Sep-Oct	2m²	60 sds

Spacing and training

Outdoors, climbing French beans are best grown up a wigwam of bamboo canes or better even hazel rods.

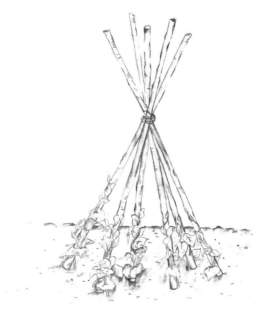

In a tunnel, climbing French beans can be grown up strings that are attached to an overhead wire. A single row in the centre of the bed with strings 30cm apart in the row and 4-5 seeds per string.

Harvesting

French and runner beans can be harvested from June (polytunnel) until the end of October (outdoor crop). The pods should be picked regularly – at least once, but twice per week is even better so they remain tender. If you stop harvesting regularly or even miss a number of pods, the plant changes its strategy and tries to mature and ripen the seeds at the expense of flowering and a longer cropping season.

Storing

French and runner beans are best eaten fresh. They are easy to blanch and freeze for the winter months and still taste quite delicious. Dried Borlotto beans will keep for a year if stored in dry conditions.

Self-sufficiency - How much to grow?

Both climbing French beans and runner beans produce an excellent yield of at least 5kg of beans per wigwam (or m²). I recommend growing 2m² of climbing French beans and 1m² of runner beans indoors early in the season and 1m² of climbing French beans and 1m² of runner beans outdoors later. If you like dried beans and have space in the polytunnel, you can grow 2m² of Borlotto beans.

Summary
A total of 5m² of climbing French and runner beans both indoors and outdoors produces 25kg of beans. If you blanch and freeze them in 500g bags, you'll get a 50-week supply of runner and French beans.

I estimate that 2m² of Borlotto beans will yield about 3-4kg of dried beans. Alternatively, you can also use runner beans, as dried beans especially if you have a glut of them.

Potential problems

Apart from slugs eating the young plants at the early stages, both runner and French beans are quite healthy and easy to grow. Make sure the climbing supports are strong enough so that they won't collapse in the summer storms.

Varieties

Climbing French beans:
Blauhild
Cobra

<u>Runner bean:</u>
Enorma
Lady Di
Scarlet Emperor

Beetroot

Beta vulgaris

Introduction

Beetroot is definitely one of the most important vegetables for the self-sufficient garden. They are so easy to grow with hardly any pests or diseases. You can also calculate exactly how many roots you need to grow. With the help of a polytunnel or greenhouse, you can get fresh beetroot for at least 11 months of the year. You can also easily preserve some roots.

There are many types of beetroot with different colours (red, orange/yellow, white and red and white striped) and shapes (round globe and cylindrical).

Soil and site

Beetroot prefers light, well-drained soil with well-rotted compost incorporated in early spring.

Sowing

Most beetroot varieties have clusters of more than one seed. This means if you sow one seed, you will have three to five seedlings germinating. These have to be thinned to one seedling as soon as they have germinated otherwise the beetroot will remain very small. The variety Pablo F1 has a monogerm seed. This means that they only contain a single seed and don't require thinning.

Seeds can be sown directly in a well-prepared seed bed in shallow drills (1.5cm deep). Alternatively, sow one seed per module and plant out 4 weeks later after hardening off.

First early beetroot in polytunnel:
Sow in modular trays in late January in heated propagator (18°C) and plant in early March in polytunnel.
Second early beetroot in polytunnel:
Sow seeds in early March directly into polytunnel beds.
Summer beetroot outdoors:
Sow seeds in mid-April directly into outdoor beds.
Maincrop/storage beetroot outdoors:
Sow seeds in late May directly into outdoor beds.

Variety	Sowing	Location	Harvest	Area	Quantity
Pablo F1	30. Jan	Polytunnel	May	1m²	40 roots
Pablo F1	1. Mar	Polytunnel	June	1m²	40 roots
Pablo F1	15. Apr	Outdoors	July - Sep	3m²	120 roots
Cylindra	20. May	Outdoors	Oct - April	3m²	120 roots
Pablo F1	20. May	Outdoors	Oct - April	4m²	160 roots

Spacing

Early crop:
Final spacing: 25cm between the rows and 10cm between plants.
Main crop:
Final spacing: 30cm between the rows and 10cm between plants.

Initially, I sow the seeds about 5cm apart. Soon after germination, thin the clusters of seedlings and just leave the strongest (not necessary for Pablo F1). When they reach the baby beetroot stage you can harvest every second plant. This allows the remaining plants to fully develop at a spacing of 10cm. If you prefer bigger roots, you can increase the spacing to 15cm between plants.

Rotation

Beetroot are a flexi-crop with no soil-borne diseases and you do not have to be too fussy about rotation.

Plant care

Apart from keeping the crop weed free and properly thinned to the required spacing, there is no other maintenance required.

Harvesting

Early summer beetroot from the polytunnel and the first outdoor crop can be harvested when required. It is best to twist off the leaves to avoid damage and bleeding of the roots.
Maincrop beetroot for storage should be left until October before harvesting.

Storing

Beetroot stores extremely well in boxes of damp sand or soil until April the following year.

Self – sufficiency - How much to grow?

It is possible to get a decent amount of beetroot for 11 months of the year from a number of sowings in the polytunnel and outdoors.

Spring beetroot - polytunnel:
At a spacing of 10cm apart in the row and 4 rows per bed, you'll get 40 beetroot per m^2. Thus, $1m^2$ sown in late January and again $1m^2$ sown in early March will produce 80 beetroots – or 10 beetroots per week over a period of 8 weeks from May to June.

Summer beetroot outdoors:
At a spacing of 10cm apart in the row and 4 rows per bed, you'll get 40 beetroot per m^2. Thus, $3m^2$ sown in mid April will produce 120 beetroots – or 10 beetroots per week over a period of 12 weeks from July to mid-September.

Winter storage beetroot outdoors:
At a spacing of 10cm apart in the row and 4 rows per bed, you'll get 40 beetroot per m^2. Thus, $7m^2$ sown at the end of May will produce 280 beetroots – or nearly 10 beetroots per week over a period of 30 weeks from mid-September to early April.

Summary
A total of $12m^2$ will produce 480 beetroots or 10 beetroot per week for 11 months.

Potential problems

There is no specific pest or disease that affects beetroot. Slugs may eat young seedlings, especially if sown too early or if the garden is a bit wild. Beetroot is sensitive to a deficiency of boron in the soil. The symptoms are brown, sunken patches on the roots and black areas inside the root. This can easily be remedied by applying a liquid boron supplement.

Varieties
Cylindra
Pablo F1
Detroit Globe

Broccoli, sprouting

Brassica oleracea Italica Group

Introduction

Sprouting broccoli is a vegetable that is sometimes confused with calabrese and sprouting seeds of broccoli. This one, however, is the real one – a large plant sown in early summer and only producing purple (and sometimes white) shoots in early spring from February to May the following year depending on variety.

As their growing season is from July/August to April/May, sprouting broccoli can be planted after a crop that is harvested in July (e.g. garlic) in the first year and then before a late planted crop such as carrots – so you'll get two crops per year.

Sprouting broccoli is an extremely useful vegetable as it matures during the hungry gap period when there are few other vegetables around. That's why it made it into the self-sufficiency list.

Soil and site

Sprouting broccoli requires a fertile, deep soil with high moisture retention and good drainage. It is easy to grow and will tolerate most sites. I recently adopted a new technique – after harvesting the preceding crop I simply hoe and rake the bed and then plant the modules. Once the plants are about 30cm tall, I add a bucket full of compost around each plant. This feeds the plants and helps to support them.

Sowing

Many beginners sow sprouting broccoli far too early and then the plants get confused and may produce in autumn or become too big to survive the winter. The best time to sow is in mid-June to mid-July. I often sow a mixture of varieties which extends the harvesting season from late January to May.

Purple sprouting broccoli can be raised in modular trays placed on a bench in a greenhouse (or tunnel). Sow one seeds per module about 1.5cm deep. They usually germinate within 7 days and are ready for planting out about 4 weeks after sowing.

Variety	Sowing	Location	Harvest	Area	Quantity
Various	25. June	Outdoors	Feb - May	4m²	6 plants

Spacing

A spacing of 75cm each way is the minimum.

Rotation

It is important to keep sprouting broccoli in the brassica section of your rotation to prevent a build up of the numerous brassica pests and diseases.

Plant care

Sprouting broccoli gets very top heavy so they will benefit from a generous earthing up. In exposed gardens, you may need to stake the plants to prevent them collapsing during winter gales.

Harvesting and storing

Harvest sprouting broccoli when the heads appear but well before they open up into yellow flowers. The plants mature around February and sometimes produce into May. The shoots should be cut when they are about 15cm long. It is absolutely crucial that they are harvested regularly at least once per week. Sprouting broccoli can be blanched and frozen.

Self – sufficiency - How much to grow?

As they fit in nicely into a rotation, there is usually sufficient space available to grow quite a number of plants. Generally, three plants are enough to produce sufficient sprouting broccoli during the harvesting season between February and May. If you grow 6 plants, you could blanch and freeze another 3 – 4 months supply of sprouting broccoli. For 6 plants you'll need 4m² of a bed.

Summary
A total of 4m² produces 0.5kg of sprouting broccoli spears per week for 4 months.

Potential problems

Sprouting broccoli is susceptible to the same pests and diseases as other brassicas.

Varieties

Purple Sprouting Early and Late
Red Arrow
Red Spear

Brussels sprouts

Brassica oleracea Gemmifera Group

Introduction

Brussels sprouts are only included in this self-sufficiency book because they are an extremely healthy vegetable and actually can produce quite a number of sprouts for quite a few months. Trust me on the variety (Brigitte F1) and the spacing and you should be able to get an amazing crop.

Soil and site

Brussels sprouts are very hardy and will grow on most sites. They should be planted in very fertile soil that has been well prepared with compost or decomposed manure.

Sowing

Brussels sprouts can be raised in modular trays placed on a bench in a greenhouse (or tunnel). Sow one seeds per module about 1.5cm deep. They usually germinate within 7 days and are ready for planting out about 4 weeks after sowing.

Autumn Brussels sprouts:

Sow in late April and plant in late May.

Winter Brussels sprouts:

Sow in mid-June and plant in mid-July.

Variety	Sowing	Location	Harvest	Area	Quantity
Brigitte F1	24. Apr	Outdoors	Oct - Dec	3m²	3 plants
Brigitte F1	15. June	Outdoors	Dec - Feb	3m²	3 plants

Spacing

Between plants: 90cm
Between rows: 90cm

This spacing appears very wide but it is the best for getting decent sprouts. At the initial stages the gaps can be intercropped with a quick maturing crop such as annual spinach, radishes, rocket or lettuce.

Rotation

It is absolutely essential to keep them in the brassica section of the rotation to prevent a build-up of the numerous brassica pests or diseases.

Plant care

On exposed sites it is beneficial to earth up the soil around the stem to prevent wind damage. Some growers on very exposed sites tie the plants to sticks. However, I believe this is rarely necessary. Any discoloured leaves should be removed from the plant on a regular basis as they may harbour pests and diseases.

Harvesting

The harvesting period can last for 5 months. Start harvesting the lower sprouts first as soon as they are big enough.

Self-sufficiency - How much to grow?

Brussels sprouts will provide a regular supply of delicious sprouts from October to February.

Autumn/winter crop outdoors:
At a spacing of 90cm apart in the row and 1 row per bed, you'll get 1 plant per m². Each plant can produce 2kg of sprouts. Thus, 3m² (3 plants) sown in late April will produce around 6kg (or 120 buds) of Brussels sprouts. You'll get around 10 buds per week over a period of 12 weeks from October to December.

Winter crop outdoors:
At a spacing of 90cm apart in the row and 1 row per bed, you'll get 1 plant per m². Each plant can produce 2kg of sprouts. Thus, 3m² (3 plants) sown in mid-June will produce around 6kg (or 120 buds) of Brussels sprouts. You'll get around 10 buds per week over a period of 12 weeks from December to February.

Summary
A total of 6m² produces 240 Brussels sprouts or over 10 buds per week for 24 weeks.

Potential problems

Brussels sprouts are susceptible to the same pests and diseases as cabbage and the same control measures are recommended. However, mealy aphids are especially a problem with sprouts in particular.

Varieties

Brigitte F1

Cabbage

Brassica oleracea Capitata Group

Introduction

Unfortunately, cabbages are no longer the most popular brassica member, having been overtaken by kale and calabrese. I think though that the good old cabbage will regain its popularity as more and more research points to its health promoting effects, especially in a fermented way. I recently started to make sauerkraut again which is far more delicious compared to the bought stuff. Nothing could be easier to make. Sauerkraut is a great way for storing cabbages and it is vital for a healthy gut microbiome.

Cabbages do extremely well in our cool, moist climate provided that plenty of compost or composted manure is available. With good planning and proper choice of varieties, it is possible to have cabbages all year round.

Soil and site

Cabbages are tolerant of cooler temperatures, but not so much to excessive heat. The optimum growing temperature is 15 – 18°C which often represents an Irish summer.
They are easy to grow and will tolerate most sites, even fairly exposed ones. Poorer soils can be improved by a heavy application of half rotted manure or compost. If the soil pH is below 6.5, you should spread calcified seaweed or ground limestone.

Sowing

Cabbages can be raised in modular trays placed on a bench in a greenhouse (or tunnel).
I sow one seed per module about 1.5cm deep.
The seeds usually germinate within 6 to 7 days and the seedlings are ready for planting out about 4 weeks after sowing.

Spring cabbage:
Sow in late January in heated propagator and plant in early March in polytunnel.
Summer cabbage:
Sow from late March to mid-April in a heated propagator at 15-18°C.
Dutch cabbage (red and white):
Sow in late April.
Hardy winter cabbage and Savoy cabbage:
Sow from mid-May to early June.

Variety	Sowing	Location	Harvest	Area	Quantity
Hispi F1	25. Jan	Polytunnel	May	1m²	12 plants
Hispi F1	25. Feb	Polytunnel	June	1m²	12 plants
Stonehead F1	1. Apr	Outdoors	July - Sep	2m²	12 plants
Rodynda	25. Apr	Outdoors	Sep - Oct	2m²	12 plants
January King	20. May	Outdoors	Oct - Apr	2m²	12 plants
Vertus	20. May	Outdoors	Oct - Apr	2m²	12 plants

Spacing

The spacing of the plants determines the size of the head. If lots of small cabbages are required, plant them closer. If you want to impress your neighbours, increase the spacing. It is a common mistake of beginners to plant cabbages far too close.

Spring cabbage (polytunnel): 25cm
Summer cabbage: 40-45cm
Autumn cabbage: 45-50cm
Dutch white & red cabbage: 45-50cm
Hardy winter cabbage: 45-50cm

Rotation

It is absolutely essential to keep cabbages in the brassica section of your rotation to prevent a build up of the numerous brassica pests and diseases.

Plant care

Regular hoeing will control weed growth whilst stimulating plant vigour.

Harvesting

With the help of the January sown spring cabbage grown in the polytunnel (and producing from May onwards), it is possible to have cabbages throughout most of the year. The summer varieties produce throughout the summer months and the winter types keep extremely well in the garden until February.

If you cut the cabbage heads a little higher up, leaving a number of outside leaves on the plant, you'll often get 3 or 4 new baby cabbages growing. These also produce a firm head and are a welcome surprise.

Storing

If you choose a good selection of varieties you should be able to get cabbages fresh from your garden nearly all year round so there is no need to store them. The firm Dutch autumn cabbages store for a month or two in a cool shed. A perfect method for using up a glut is to make sauerkraut.

Self – sufficiency - How much to grow?

Cabbages are not a profitable crop for a market gardener but they certainly are for a smallholder. They do take up a lot of space in the garden but they also produce a heavy yield.

Early spring cabbage polytunnel crop:
At a spacing of 25cm apart in the row and 3 rows per bed, you'll get 12 cabbages per m². As soon as the growing plants touch each other I harvest every second plant as spring greens (non-hearted leafy cabbage) and to give the remaining plants space to bulk up.
Thus, 1m² sown in late January and again in late February will produce 3 spring greens or spring cabbages per week over a period of 8 weeks from May to June.

Summer cabbages outdoors:

At a spacing of 45cm apart in the row and 3 rows per bed, you'll get 6 cabbages per m². Thus, 2m² sown in early April will produce 12 cabbages.

You'll get 1 cabbage per week over a period of 12 weeks from July to September.

Dutch cabbage (Rodynda):

At a spacing of 45cm apart in the row and 3 rows per bed, you'll get 6 cabbages per m². Thus, 2m² sown in late April will produce 12 cabbages.

You'll get 1 cabbage per week over a period of 12 weeks from September to November.

Winter cabbages outdoors:

At a spacing of 45cm apart in the row and 3 rows per bed, you'll get 6 cabbages per m². Thus, 4m² sown in late May will produce 24 cabbages.

You'll get 1 cabbage per week over a period of 20 weeks from October to February.

There will be a few spare for friends and also remember to leave the stalk for the small bonus cabbages.

Summary

A total of 8m² produces 72 cabbages or 1.5 cabbages per week for 10 months.

Potential problems

Cabbages are susceptible to the same insect and disease pests as all the other brassicas and the same control measures as for other brassicas are recommended.

Varieties

Spring cabbage:
Hispi F1
Pyramid F1
Summer cabbage:
Stonehead F1
Winter cabbage:
January King
Celtic F1
Savoy cabbage:
Vertus
Dutch cabbage:
Rodynda (red)
Dottenfelder Dauer

Calabrese

Brassica oleracea Italica Group

Introduction

Calabrese (commonly called broccoli) produces a central large green head followed by a number of smaller spears emerging after the main head was cut. Each plant will produce smaller heads for at least 6 weeks.

Sowing

Calabrese needs to be sown in succession to ensure a long harvesting season and to minimise gluts. I always sow calabrese in modular trays which are placed in a greenhouse. I sow one seed per module about 1.5cm deep. They usually germinate within 6 to 7 days and are ready for planting out about 4 weeks after sowing.

Variety	Sowing	Location	Harvest	Area	Quantity
Tiara F1	25. Jan	Polytunnel	Apr - May	1m²	6 heads
Tiara F1	1. Mar	Polytunnel	May - June	1m²	6 heads
Chevalier F1	20. Mar	Outdoors	June - July	1m²	6 heads
Chevalier F1	20. Apr	Outdoors	July - Aug	1m²	6 heads
Chevalier F1	20. May	Outdoors	Aug - Sep	1m²	6 heads
Chevalier F1	15. June	Outdoors	Sep - Oct	1m²	6 heads
Chevalier F1	10. July	Polytunnel	Oct	1m²	6 heads
Chevalier F1	10. Aug	Polytunnel	Nov	1m²	6 heads

Spacing

I recommend a spacing of 45cm apart in the row and 3 rows per bed. This spacing will produce a medium–sized central head followed by numerous smaller spears.

Rotation

It is absolutely essential to keep calabrese in the brassica section of your rotation to prevent a build-up of the numerous brassica pests and diseases.

Plant care

Calabrese requires plenty of water at all stages. The plants benefit from a top-dressing of organic poultry manure pellets (a small handful per plant) after the central head is cut in order to encourage side shoots.

Harvesting

The central head should be cut before the flowers open. Smaller side shoots will develop later and you can expect at least three further cuts. Generally cropping may start about 70 to 100 days after sowing depending on the variety and season.

Storing

Calabrese is best eaten fresh. However, if you have a glut the heads can be blanched and frozen.

Self – sufficiency - How much to grow?

At a spacing of 45cm apart in the row and 3 rows per bed, you'll get 6 calabrese heads per m^2 (followed by numerous smaller shoots). Thus, 8m^2 sown in succession from late January to August (both for growing in a polytunnel and outdoors) will produce 48 heads or calabrese plus side shoots from late April to early November.

You'll get 2 calabrese heads and side shoots per week over a period of 24 weeks from late April to early November.

Summary
A total of 8m^2 produces 48 calabrese heads or 2 heads per week for 6 months.

Potential problems

Calabrese is susceptible to the same pests and diseases as cabbage and the same control measures are recommended. The main problem with calabrese is premature flowering. It is absolutely crucial to check your plants for ripeness at least twice per week. The flower buds open up into yellow flowers so quickly and become useless.

Varieties:

Chevalier F1
Marathon F1
Tiara F1

Carrot

Daucus carota var. *sativus*

Introduction

Carrots are one of the healthy staple crops and deserve a little extra attention in your garden. They are not always the easiest crop to grow. The two main problems are slugs or snails eating the little seedlings just as they appear and before the gardener even notices the problem, and secondly the dreaded carrot rootfly. If you had problems with carrot root fly in the past you will need to cover the crop with a specialised carrot root fly netting (e.g. bionet or enviromesh).

Soil and site

Early crops prefer a more sheltered spot while maincrop carrots thrive better on an open site. Carrots do best on light and stone free soil with good drainage. Never add fresh manure to the soil before sowing carrots. Well-rotted compost is best incorporated into the soil in the autumn and the soil should then be covered with black plastic over the winter to prevent leaching of nutrients.

Sowing

Carrots require a very fine seedbed and even under ideal conditions they take about 2 weeks to germinate. Seeds should be sown about 2cm deep in shallow drills and thinned to the required spacing. If you manage to sow them evenly there is no need to thin the crop. Never transplant carrots or grow them in modules.

Weed control is essential in the early stages of growth to get the plants established. Watch out for slugs 2 to 3 weeks after sowing and use organic slug pellets if needed.

First early carrots in polytunnel:
Sow seeds in late January directly into polytunnel beds. Beds can be pre-warmed by placing a sheet of plastic onto the soil for 4 weeks before sowing.
Second early carrots in polytunnel:
Sow seeds in early March directly into polytunnel beds.
Summer carrots outdoors:
Sow seeds in mid-April directly into outdoor beds.
Maincrop/storage carrots outdoors:
Sow seeds in late May directly into outdoor beds.

Variety	Sowing	Location	Harvest	Area	Quantity
Amsterdam	30. Jan	Polytunnel	May	2m²	160 roots
Nantes	1. Mar	Polytunnel	June	2m²	160 roots
Romance F1	15. Apr	Outdoors	July- Sep	3m²	240 roots
Romance F1	31. May	Outdoors	Oct- Apr	7m²	560 roots

Spacing

Between plants: 4-5cm
Between rows: 20-25cm

Rotation

Carrots should be grown with the other members of the Umbellifer family. It is important that carrots are rotated.

Plant care

Carrots should be kept well-weeded at all times because they are bad competitors with weeds.

If carrot rootfly is a problem in your garden, keep the bionet cloche on throughout the entire growing season and check regularly that there are no gaps. Grow your early, outdoor carrots under a separate bionet cloche than the maincrop carrots. The cloche of your maincrop carrots should only be opened very briefly to hoe and weed. No maincrop carrot should be pulled as the smell would attract the rootfly.

Harvesting

Early carrots can be pulled small as required. Grow the early carrots under a separate bionet cloche than the maincrop. Maincrop carrots should be harvested in October. Please refrain from pulling carrots from the maincrop as you would attract the carrot rootfly. Maincrop carrots should be harvested all in one go otherwise the carrot root fly will be attracted by the smell. Twist off the leaves and store.

Storing

Carrots are ideally stored in a box of moist sand or soil in a cool frost free shed. Before storage, grading is essential. Any roots with carrot fly damage or diseases should not be stored with the healthy ones. Carrots will keep until April. You may have to go through the box and sort them – they may produce new shoots or roots. These need to be rubbed off and then placed back into the box with sand/soil.

Self-sufficiency - How much to grow?

Carrots are likely to be the most important crop for the self-sufficient garden. With the help of a polytunnel it is possible to get carrots nearly all-year-round.

Early spring polytunnel crops:
At a spacing of 5cm apart in the row and 4 rows per bed, you'll get 80 carrots per m². Thus, 2m² sown in late January and again 2m² in early March will produce about 320 carrots or 40 carrots per week over a period of 8 weeks in May and June. The first early pickings will be quite small.

<u>Summer/autumn crop outdoors:</u>
At a spacing of 5cm apart in the row and 4 rows per bed, you'll get 80 carrots per m². Thus, 3m² sown in mid-April will produce about 240 carrots or 20 carrots per week over a period of 12 weeks in July to September.

<u>Winter storage crop outdoors:</u>
At a spacing of 5cm apart in the row and 4 rows per bed, you'll get 80 carrots per m². Thus, 6m² sown in late May will produce about 560 carrots or 18 carrots per week over a period of 30 weeks from October to April.

Summary
A total of 14m² produces over 1,000 carrots or 20 carrots per week for 12 months of the year.

Twenty carrots per week seems like a lot of food, but with carrots you'll never know what happens and this is a nice buffer.

Varieties

Amsterdam Forcing (early)

Early Nantes (early)

Autumn King

Chantenay Red Cored

Nairobi F1

Napoli F1

Romance F1

Celeriac

Apium graveolens var. *rapaceum*

Introduction

Celeriac is an excellent winter vegetable but rather difficult to grow. It needs a long growing season and can be eaten raw or cooked. It is grown for its crisp, celery-flavoured root which really is a swollen stem - a staple in Europe, but little more than a novelty in Ireland.

Soil and site

Celeriac likes a sheltered garden and a rich, loamy soil with plenty of well-rotted compost added to it.

Sowing and planting

In the third week in March, broadcast the seeds into a standard seed tray or pot containing seed compost. The seeds should not be covered as they need light to germinate. Move the trays onto a propagator (18°C) or a south-facing window-sill.

Celeriac may take between 2 to 3 weeks to germinate. They can be pricked out into modular trays about 2 weeks after germination. Harden off the seedlings before planting out about 8 weeks after sowing around the third week in May.

Spacing

Plants should be spaced 35 x 35cm each way.

Rotation

Celeriac should be rotated along with other Umbellifers.

Plant care

Plants are shallow-rooted and require consistent moisture so be careful when hoeing because of their shallow roots. They will benefit from a top-dressing of well-decomposed compost or poultry pellets in the summer and water during dry spells. In summer remove the outer leaves to expose the crown and encourage the bulb to develop.

Harvesting and storing

The roots can be harvested from October onwards. They can either be stored in boxes of sand or in mild districts they can be left in the ground and harvested as required.

Self – sufficiency - How much to grow?

If you eat 2 celeriac roots per week (Season: October until March - 24 weeks), you will need 48 celeriac plants.
At a spacing of 35cm apart in the row and 3 rows per bed, you'll get 9 celeriac roots per m².

In 5 metres you will get enough celeriac for 24 weeks.

Summary
A total of 5m² will produce 45 celeriac roots or 2 celeriac roots per week for 6 months.

Varieties

Giant Prague
Mars

Celery

Apium graveolens L. var. _dulce_

Introduction

Celery has become very popular in recent years but, unfortunately, it is one of the more difficult vegetables to grow. The secret of growing good celery is to sow it correctly, choose a good variety (Victoria F1) and grow it on a fertile, moisture-retentive soil. With the help of a polytunnel it is possible to produce your own celery from June to November.

If celery is grown for home consumption only, there is no need to harvest the whole head. You can simply twist off individual leaves from the outside of the plant.

Soil and site

Celery likes a sheltered garden and prefers a rich, loamy soil with plenty of well-rotted compost added to it. It's originally a wetland plant – so it likes any additional moisture.

Sowing

Broadcast the seeds into a standard seed tray or pot, containing seed compost. The seeds should not be covered as they need light to germinate. The trays should be placed in a warm place, either on a windowsill or in a propagator.

Celery may take between 2 to 3 weeks to germinate. Around 10 - 14 days after germination, prick the seedling out and transfer them into modular trays. Harden off the seedlings before planting out about 8 weeks after sowing.

First early celery in polytunnel:
Sow seeds in mid-February in pots on the heating bench (18°C), prick out into modular trays in mid-March and plant into polytunnel in mid-April.

Second early celery in polytunnel:
Sow seeds in late March in pots on heating bench (18°C), prick out into modular trays in late April and plant into polytunnel in late May.
Summer celery outdoors:
Sow seeds in early April in pots on heating bench (18°C), prick out into modular trays in early May and plant outdoors in early June.
Late celery in polytunnel:
Sow seeds in early June in pots, prick out into modular trays in early July and plant into polytunnel in early August.

Variety	Sowing	Location	Harvest	Area	Quantity
Victoria F1	15. Feb	Polytunnel	May - June	1m²	12 plants
Victoria F1	31. Mar	Polytunnel	June - Aug	1m²	12 plants
Victoria F1	10. Apr	Outdoors	Aug - Sep	1m²	12 plants
Victoria F1	10. June	Polytunnel	Oct - Nov	1m²	12 plants

Spacing

Plant celery at a spacing of 27 x 27cm each way.

Rotation

Celery should be rotated along with the other Umbellifers.

Plant care

Plants are shallow-rooted and require consistent moisture. Lack of water will make the stalks fibrous and bitter. The plants should be kept weed-free and moist at all times.

Harvesting

Celery can be harvested from May until November with early and late crops grown with protection.

You can harvest the whole plant when the stalks are reasonably big and before they get stringy. If you don't cut the plant too low and leave it in the ground you'll find that a number of new celery shoots will appear within a few days. These will produce a second crop about three weeks later.

Alternatively, you can harvest individual stalks from the outside of the plant and it will keep producing new stalks from the centre. With this technique you can harvest at least 2 stalks/plant/week for quite a number of weeks.

Self – sufficiency - How much to grow?

If you need 24 celery stalks (leaves) per week (Season: May to mid-November - 26 weeks) you will need 48 celery plants.

At a spacing of 27cm apart in the row and 4 rows per bed, you'll get 12 celery plants per m^2.

When harvesting 2 stalks per plant per week you'll get 24 stalks per week per m^2.

In 4 m^2, you will get enough celery for 26 weeks.

Summary

A total of 4m^2 will produce 48 celery plants or 24 celery stalks per week for 6.5 months.

Potential problems

Young plants need to be protected from slugs. The celery leaf miner (also known as the celery fly) may sometimes cause damage. The symptoms include blistering of the leaves.

Varieties

Lathom Blanching Galaxy
Victoria F1

Courgette & Marrow

Cucurbita pepo

Introduction

Courgettes and marrows are the ideal crop for the self-sufficient garden. They produce an enormous amount of food – a wonderful gift of nature. A small number of plants are sufficient to give you a fairly large amount of courgettes during their season. They are a big contender for the value-for-space competition.

Courgettes are young, immature fruits and when left to grow, they turn into marrows.

Soil and site

Courgettes need a fertile, free-draining soil which can hold plenty of moisture. A generous application of well-decomposed compost is essential. They also need a sheltered place in the garden as they really dislike strong wind.

Sowing

Sow seeds individually into 7cm pots. Ideally, the pots are left in a propagator in the greenhouse.
After about 3-4 weeks, pot them on into 12cm pots which are left in the greenhouse or indoors.

Variety	Sowing	Location	Harvest	Area	Quantity
Green /Yellow	15. Mar	Polytunnel	May - Aug	3m²	3 plants
Green /Yellow	25. Apr	Outdoors	July - Sep	3m²	3 plants
Green /Yellow	15. June	Polytunnel	Sep – Nov	3m²	3 plants

Spacing

The ideal planting distance is 1m between plants. It is important to stick to this spacing, but you can interplant some lettuce or annual spinach into the gaps.

These can be harvested before the courgettes require the full space.

Rotation

Courgettes belong to the cucurbit family. This family is not prone to any soil-borne pests and diseases, so you do not need to be too fussy with rotations.

Plant care

Apart from regular harvesting and keeping the weeds down, there is very little else to do. Remove any overgrown fruits as these drain the energy from the plant and thus, reduce yield.

Harvesting

Harvest courgettes as soon as they are the size you require. In fact, you may have to harvest them about 3 times per week, especially in the tunnel.

Storing

Courgettes do not store for more than a week in the fridge, but marrows will last for about 3 months in a cool, but frost-free, building.

Self – sufficiency - How much to grow?

From each courgette plant you will get a minimum of 2 courgettes per week for 3-4 months.

First sowing (for polytunnel), in mid-March - 3m² - gives you 6 courgettes per week from May to August.

Second sowing (for outdoors), in late April - 3m² - gives you 6 courgettes per week from July to September.

Third sowing (for polytunnel), in mid-June - 3m² - gives you 6 courgettes per week from September to November.

Summary
A total of 9m² will produce around 240 courgettes or on average 8 courgettes per week for 7 months.

Potential problems

There are very few problems with courgettes. The main problem occurs if you plant them out too early. The plants will be damaged by strong, cold winds or die in the first light frost. During the end of the season, plants will get attacked by powdery mildew. There is no cure for it but it does not kill the plant.

Varieties

Ambassador F1
Defender F1
Nero di Milano
Parador F1 (yellow)

Cucumber

Cucumis sativus

Introduction

Cucumbers are warmth-loving plants so they can only be grown in a polytunnel or greenhouse. It is probably one of the most productive plants for the self-sufficient garden. Cucumbers grow very quickly, but they can also die quickly if conditions are wrong.

Soil and site

Cucumbers love warmth, high humidity and very high soil fertility. Just imagine a plant that grows to well over 2m² tall and produces such a prolific crop!

Incorporate plenty of very well-rotted compost or manure into the beds about a month before planting.

Sowing

Only sow an "all female" F1 hybrid variety of cucumber. Open pollinated varieties have both male and female flowers which produce bitter, tough skinned fruits, full of hard seeds and with a "belly" at the end.

As cucumbers are warmth-loving crops, I delay sowing until the third week in April and make a second sowing in late May/early June.

Sow seeds individually into small pots (7cm) and place the pots into a propagator (21°C). The seeds germinate quickly within 5 to 6 days. About 2 to 3 weeks after sowing the plants are ready to be potted on into a bigger pot (12cm) using a more fertile potting compost. Keep the pots on the heating bench or on a south-facing window sill in the house until planting.

Variety	Sowing	Location	Harvest	Area	Quantity
Passandra F1	20. Apr	Polytunnel	Jun - Aug	1m²	2 plants
Passandra F1	1. June	Polytunnel	Aug– Oct	1m²	2 plants

Planting

When the plants are well rooted in the 12cm pots they can be planted into their final growing position in the greenhouse or polytunnel. I train the plants up strings that are attached to an overhead wire, so when I plant them I first dig a big enough planting hole and then lay the bottom part of the string into the hole with the end sticking up, then take the cucumber plant out of the pot and place it over the string and gently firm them in. Do not plant cucumbers too deep, this reduces the risk of stem rot.

Spacing

Plants can be spaced 50cm apart in the row and only a single row should be planted per bed.

Plant care

Just remember, cucumbers need a tropical environment so regular misting with warm water especially during the day is highly beneficial. On a weekly basis you should gently wind the main stem of the plant around the upright string and remove all side shoots. All the fruit from the bottom 30cm should be removed while still small. This early fruit removal enables the plants to grow stronger. Feed the plants organic poultry manure pellets in July – around one hand-full per plant.

Harvesting

There are few things that are more impressive than the yield of cucumbers. Every day, each plant produces a new cucumber during the high season. It is important that you harvest the crop regularly or otherwise the plants will stop producing.

Storing

My mother always made the most delicious cucumber pickle. Instead of using gherkins, she used cucumbers. This is a great method of using up your gluts.

Self – sufficiency – How much to grow?

From each cucumber plant you will get a minimum of 5 cucumbers per week for 3-4 months.

First sowing (for polytunnel) in mid April - 1m² (2 plants) - gives you 10 cucumbers per week from June to August.

Second sowing (for polytunnel) in early June - 1m² (2 plants) - gives you 10 cucumbers per week from August to October.

Summary
A total of 2m² (4 plants) will produce around 240 cucumbers or 10 cucumbers per week for 5 months.

Potential problems

Frost damage, red spider mite and stem rots.
To prevent these problems – start the plants later in the season, spray the plants with warm water on a warm day and don't plant too deep.

Varieties

Passandra F1 (medium sized)

Garlic

Allium sativum

Introduction

Garlic is one of my favourite vegetables. It can be grouped into autumn and spring planted garlic. Here are a few tips on how to grow great garlic:
- Give them plenty of space – at least 20 or 25cm between plants.
- Grow a good variety and plant only first class bulbs (discard any rubbish).
- If your soil is heavy, grow garlic in raised beds.

There are softneck and hardneck varieties available and both are excellent. Hardneck varieties appear as if they have bolted, but garlic doesn't bolt. These hard flower stalks are also called garlic scapes and are edible as well. Some cooks rate them as delicacies. The scapes can be harvested about 3 weeks before harvesting the bulbs. Only use the top half and leave the remainder on the plant.

Green or immature garlic is a vegetable in itself and has risen in popularity in recent years. You simply harvest the whole plant before the bulb starts to form and eat them like a deliciously garlic-flavoured vegetable similar to leeks.

Soil and site

Garlic prefers a light, free draining soil. If the soil is heavy, make raised beds and incorporate well-decomposed compost. It is essential that garlic is grown in full sun.

Planting

Garlic is grown by planting individual cloves which are split off from the bulb. On average, there are around ten cloves per bulb. In order to get decent sized bulbs, plant the cloves at least 20 - 25cm apart each way. The cloves are planted upright with the tips about 2cm below the surface. Garlic generally requires a cold period of about 6 weeks at a temperature below 7°C. This is the reason why garlic has to be planted in autumn or very early spring. If it is planted too late individual cloves won't develop and you will be left with a solid, clove-less bulb.

Autumn planting:
Plant cloves outdoors or in a polytunnel from late September until early November.

Spring planting:
Spring planting is more advisable if the ground is too wet in winter. Plant cloves outdoors from February until early April.

Variety	Sowing	Location	Harvest/Store	Area	Qty
Various	15. Oct	Polytunnel	Late May - June	1m²	16 bulbs
Various	15. Oct	Outdoors	July - Feb	4m²	64 bulbs
Various	20. Feb	Outdoors	Aug - Mar	2m²	32 bulbs

Spacing

Between plants: 20 - 25cm
Between rows: 25cm

Rotation

It is important to rotate garlic. It can only return to the same plot after 4 years otherwise you may encounter a build up of soil-borne diseases such as white rot. If you ever get white rot in your garden, you will be unable to grow garlic or any relative for the next 10 years.

Plant Care

Keep the plot weed-free.

Harvesting and storing

Garlic is ready to harvest when leaves turn yellow-brown. Unlike onions, harvest garlic before the stalks fall over. This is important, otherwise the bulb opens up and won't store as well. Dig the bulbs out carefully with a fork. Remove excess dirt from the root, but never cut off the foliage.

Ideally, garlic should ideally be dried in the sun for 3-4 weeks. As this is generally not possible in Ireland, dry the bulbs in an airy open shed.

When the garlic is fully dried, it can be tied into bunches. If braiding, do so while tops still have moisture and are flexible. The longer the tops stay on, the longer the storage life. Air movement is essential. Store as cool and dry as possible. The lower the temperature, the longer the storage life.

Storage at high temperatures (e.g. room temperature) is satisfactory but for shorter periods.

Self – sufficiency - How much to grow?

At a spacing of 25cm apart in the row and 4 rows per bed, you'll get 16 garlic bulbs per m². First planting in October (polytunnel) - 1m² (16 bulbs) - gives you 4 garlic bulbs per week in late May - June.

Second planting in October (outdoors) - 4m² (64 bulbs) - gives you 2 garlic bulbs per week from July to February.

Third planting in February (outdoors) - 2m² (32 bulbs) - gives you 1 garlic bulb per week from August to March.

Summary

A total of 7m² will produce 112 garlic bulbs or 2.5 garlic bulbs per week for 10 months. This will surely keep you fit and healthy.

Potential problems

Garlic is susceptible to the same diseases as onion.

Varieties

Carcassone Wight (hardneck)
Early Purple Wight (softneck)
Picardy Wight (softneck
Provence Wight (softneck)
Sultop (hardneck)
Vallelado (softneck)

Unusual variety:
Elephant garlic (*Allium ampeloprasum*):
It is actually a form of leek even if it forms cloves that resemble garlic, but the appearance and flavour resemble leeks.

Kale

Brassica oleracea Acephala Group

Introduction

Kale is one of the hardiest winter vegetables and one of the easiest to grow. It has gained popularity like no other crop. It used to be a crop for the cold winter months but now people use it all year round. From a small area you'll get a regular supply of fresh and healthy kale leaves.

Soil and site

Kale prefers a fertile, deep soil with high moisture retention. A generous amount of compost or composted manure will increase its yield substantially.

Sowing

Kale can be raised in modular trays placed on a bench in a greenhouse (or tunnel). I sow one seed per module about 1.5cm deep.

They usually germinate within 6 to 7 days (at 18°C) and seedlings are ready for planting out about 4 weeks after sowing.

Spring kale polytunnel crop:
Sow in late January in heated propagator (18°C) and plant in early March in polytunnel.
Summer/autumn kale:
Sow from late March to mid-April in a heated propagator at 15-18°C and plant outdoors.
Autumn/winter kale:
Sow in late April and plant outdoors.
Winter/spring kale:
Sow in early June and plant outdoors.
Winter/spring kale polytunnel crop:
Sow in early September and plant in polytunnel

Variety	Sowing	Location	Harvest	Area	Quantity
various	25. Jan	Polytunnel	April/May	1m²	9 plants
various	1. April	Outdoors	June - Aug	1m²	6 plants
various	28. Apr	Outdoors	Aug - Nov	1m²	6 plants
various	3. June	Outdoors	Oct - Feb	1m²	6 plants
various	1. Sep	Polytunnel	Dec- April	1m²	9 plants

Spacing

The spacing of the plants determines the size of the plants and the size of the kale leaves. Traditionally, I would space the plants about 45cm x 35cm (6 plants/m²). Most people, however, prefer much smaller leaves – so a spacing of 30cm x 30cm (9 plants/m²) may be more suitable.

In the polytunnel, I space the plants at 9 plants/m² and outdoors at 6 plants/m².

Rotation

It is essential to keep cabbages in the brassica section of your rotation to prevent a build up of the numerous brassica pests and diseases.

Plant care

Regular hoeing will control weed growth whilst stimulating plant vigour.

Harvesting

It is possible to get fresh kale all year round from your garden and polytunnel. Any variety can be used for different planting dates. Always harvest the bottom leaves first. You can harvest 2 to 3 leaves per plant each time but you should always leave the top 7 to 8 leaves to grow on.

Self-sufficiency - How much to grow?

If you eat kale regularly, 1m² (per sowing) are sufficient. If you only require a few leaves for the occasional meal a couple of plants will be sufficient.

Early spring polytunnel crop:
At a spacing of 30cm apart in the row and 3 rows per bed, you'll get 9 kale plants per m². Thus, 1m² sown in late January will produce about 0.5kg of kale leaves per week over a period of 8 weeks from April - May.

Summer/autumn crop outdoors:
At a spacing of 45cm apart in the row and 3 rows per bed, you'll get 6 kale plants per m². Thus, 1m² sown in early April will produce 0.5kg of kale leaves per week over a period of 12 weeks from June to August.

Autumn/winter crop outdoors:
At a spacing of 45cm apart in the row and 3 rows per bed, you'll get 6 kale plants per m². Thus, 1m² sown in late April will produce 0.5kg of kale leaves per week over a period of 16 weeks from August to November.

Winter/spring crop outdoors:
At a spacing of 45cm apart in the row and 3 rows per bed, you'll get 6 kale plants per m². Thus, 1m² sown in early June will produce 0.5kg of kale leaves per week over a period of 20 weeks from October to February.

Winter/spring crop in polytunnel:
At a spacing of 30cm apart in the row and 3 rows per bed, you'll get 9 kale plants per m². Thus, 1m² sown in early September will produce 0.5kg of kale leaves per week over a period of 20 weeks from December to April.

Summary
A total of 5m² produces over 0.5kg of kale leaves per week for 12 months of the year.

Potential problems

Kale is the easiest and healthiest brassica you can grow. It will suffer from all the common brassica problems, but generally to a much lesser extent.

Varieties

Nero de Toscana
Pentland Brig
Redbor F1
Red Russian
Winterbor F1

Leek

Allium porrum, or *ampeloprasum*

Introduction

The leek is a popular winter vegetable and, with a choice of different varieties, the season can be extended by many months. It's an easy vegetable to grow and also very prolific. You'll get a lot of food from a small area.

Soil and site

Leeks prefer an open site with deep, fertile, loamy soil, enriched with plenty of farmyard manure or compost.

Sowing

There are various methods of sowing leeks. The following is my preferred method. It's a little more time-consuming, but fool-proof and it'll produce leeks with nice long shanks.
I sow 2 seeds per cell in a modular seed tray. About 4 weeks later I plant the seedling out into an outdoor seedbed (or polytunnel if you have space) which is well-prepared. Seedlings are planted into a 10cm furrow in the seedbed about 5cm apart. Apart from hoeing (and thus levelling the furrow), I can forget about them until they are pencil-thick (after a further 4-6 weeks). Then they are planted into their final position about 15cm apart – again into furrows that will later be levelled and then earthed up. This allows the leeks to develop the nice long white shank. Where the soil touches the stem it blanches it and makes it more tender.

Autumn/winter leeks outdoors:
Sow in early March in heated propagator, plant in outdoor seedbed in early April and plant into final position in May. Sow an autumn and winter variety on the same date.

<u>Spring leeks outdoors:</u>
Sow from late May, plant in outdoor seedbed in late June and plant into final position in late July.

Variety	Sowing	Location	Harvest	Area	Quantity
Hannibal	1. Mar	Outdoors	Aug- Nov	2m²	36 plants
Bluegreen Winter	1. Mar	Outdoors	Nov - Feb	2m²	36 plants
Blue Solaise	20. May	Outdoors	Mar - May	2m²	36 plants

Planting

Leeks should be planted deeply – up to where the leaves divide. Do not trim the roots as research has shown that this method lowers the yield. Shortening the leaves at planting can be done if too long and floppy.

Spacing

Between plants: 15cm
Between rows: 45cm

Rotation

It is essential to adhere to a strict rotation with leeks. They should be rotated along with the other alliums.

Plant care

As the plants grow, earth up the leeks with soil to blanch the stems. This means the covered part of the leek turns white. Be careful that you don't get soil into the heart of the leek. Generally, I earth them up twice during the growing season.

Harvesting

Early varieties may be ready in late summer to late autumn. Late varieties are very hardy and can be harvested right through the winter until spring.

Self – sufficiency - How much to grow?

It is possible to get leeks for 9 months of the year from outdoor crops with just two sowing dates. If well grown, they are the most satisfying crop.

Summer/autumn leeks outdoors:
At a spacing of 15cm apart in the row and 3 rows per bed, you'll get 18 leeks per m². Thus, 2m² sown in early March will produce 36 leeks. You'll get 2 leeks per week over a period of 18 weeks from August to November.

Winter leeks outdoors:
At a spacing of 15cm apart in the row and 3 rows per bed, you'll get 18 leeks per m². Thus, 2m² sown in early March will produce 36 leeks. You'll get 2 leeks per week over a period of 18 weeks from November to February.

Winter/spring leeks outdoors:
At a spacing of 15cm apart in the row and 3 rows per bed, you'll get 18 leeks per m². Thus, 2m² sown in late May will produce 36 leeks. You'll get 3 leeks per week over a period of 12 weeks from March to May.

Summary
A total of 6m² produces 108 leeks or 2 to 3 leeks per week for 9 to 10 months.

Potential problems

Leeks are relatively trouble free. Rust is, however, an increasingly common problem but won't kill the crop. Leeks may also suffer from the general allium diseases such as white rot, but they are really a lot more resistant than onions.

Varieties

Bluegreen Winter (winter)
Blue Solaise (spring)
Hannibal (autumn)

Lettuce

Lactuca sativa

Introduction

Lettuce is without doubt the world's most popular salad plant. By careful selection of varieties and successional sowings (for the polytunnel and outdoors), you can harvest fresh lettuce for at least 8 months of the year. There are many types of lettuce – butterhead, crisphead, cos, loose-leaf and batavia.

Please note that rocket, mizuna, mustards or cresses belong to the brassica family and are not covered in this section.

Soil and site

Lettuce grows well in any reasonable garden soil. Half a bucket of well-rotted garden compost per square meter is sufficient.

Sowing

Many lettuce varieties fail to germinate when the compost temperature is above 25°C. This is important to remember because these temperatures often occur even in spring and summer if your plants are raised in trays in a tunnel. During hot spells, move the trays into a cool shed for 2 days, and then back into the tunnel. At 18°C lettuce will germinate after 3-4 days.

I generally sow lettuce seeds in modular trays. If I want a head of lettuce, only one seed per cell is required. For cut and come again lettuce, I generally sow 3 seeds per cell. Lettuce needs light to germinate, so do not cover the seeds with compost.

Timing:
From sowing to planting out: 3-5 weeks depending on the season and the weather. From planting to harvesting: 4-6 weeks.

Spring lettuce for polytunnel:
Sow in early February and early March in heated propagator (18°C) and plant out about 5 weeks later in the polytunnel.

Summer lettuce for outdoors:
Sow from early April to early August and plant out 4 weeks later outdoors.

Autumn lettuce for polytunnel:
Sow in early August and plant out 4 weeks later in polytunnel.

Hardy winter lettuce for polytunnel:
Sow in early September and plant out 4 weeks later in polytunnel (for harvesting in the following spring).

Variety	Sowing	Location	Harvest	Area	Quantity
Various	1. Feb	Polytunnel	May	1m²	16 lettuces
Various	1. Mar	Polytunnel	June	1m²	16 lettuces
Various	1. Apr	Outdoors	June	1m²	16 lettuces
Various	1. May	Outdoors	July	1m²	16 lettuces
Various	1. June	Outdoors	Aug	1m²	16 lettuces
Various	1. July	Outdoors	Sept	1m²	16 lettuces
Various	1. Aug	Outdoors	Oct	1m²	16 lettuces
Various	1. Aug	Polytunnel	Oct	1m²	16 lettuces
Various	1. Sep	Polytunnel	Mar	1m²	16 lettuces

Planting

Harden off seedlings before planting outdoors or plant under bionet cloche which should be left for a week or two over the newly planted crops until they are settled in. The seedlings should be planted with their seed leaves (cotyledons) just above ground level.

If your seedlings do get a bit leggy, you can safely plant them a little bit deeper in order to cover the stem but only up to the seed leaves. The plants definitely seem to appreciate this extra care.

Never plant the seedling deeper. If the growth point of the plant is buried, it will rot away.

Spacing

Small lettuce (Little Gem)
Between plants: 20cm
Between rows: 20cm

Medium lettuce (Lollo types, butterheads etc)
Between plants: 25cm
Between rows: 25cm

Rotation

Lettuce is an ideal plant for filling gaps in your vegetable plot e.g. plant between widely spaced crops such as kale or Brussels sprouts. The lettuce can be harvested before the main plant needs the space. If you have any spare space anywhere in your garden, you can happily plant lettuce there. Try not to plant lettuce in the same spot the following year to prevent a build up of pests and diseases.

Plant care

It is important to keep your lettuces weed free at all times and avoid spilling earth onto the leaves while weeding. During dry spells, you may have to water the plants.

Harvesting and storing

I think, with lettuce, you will often have the same problem. It is either a feast or a famine. They nearly always ripen at the same time and quickly go into flower. You can pick leaves from the leafy lettuces as soon as they are of a usable size. You can also cut loose leaf lettuce about 5cm above the base of the lettuce and the plant will send out new leaves which can be cut again about 2 to 3 weeks later.

Harvest lettuce very early in the morning as it will keep much better.

Self – sufficiency - How much to grow?

It is possible to get lettuce for 7-8 months of the year from polytunnel and outdoor crops. A monthly, successional sowing should be sufficient.

Early spring lettuce - polytunnel:
At a spacing of 25cm apart in the row and 4 rows per bed, you'll get 16 lettuces per m². Thus, 1m² sown in late January and again 1m² sown in early February will produce 4 lettuces per week over a period of 8 weeks from May to June.

Summer lettuces outdoors:
At a spacing of 25cm apart in the row and 4 rows per bed, you'll get 16 lettuces per m². Thus, 1m² sown in early April and repeated monthly until early August, will produce 4 to 5 lettuces per week over a period of 16 weeks from July to October.

Autumn lettuce – polytunnel crop:
At a spacing of 25cm apart in the row and 4 rows per bed, you'll get 16 lettuces per m². Thus, 1m² sown in early August will produce 4 lettuces per week over a period of 4 weeks in October.

Spring lettuce – polytunnel crop:
At a spacing of 25cm apart in the row and 4 rows per bed, you'll get 16 lettuces per m². Thus, 1m² sown in early September will produce 4 lettuces per week over a period of 4 weeks in mid March to mid-April.

Summary
A total of 9m² produces 144 heads of lettuce or 4 to 5 lettuces per week for 8 months. This is only a rough guideline.
Instead of harvesting the entire head of lettuce you can prolong the growing season by harvesting individual leaves or use the cut-and-come-again technique.

Potential problems

Pests:
Leatherjackets, wireworm, cutworms, slugs and snails, leaf aphids, root aphids
Diseases:
Downy mildew (Bremia) and grey mould (Botrytis).
Disorders:
Tip burn

Varieties

Aruba
Batavia (red and green)
Marvel of Four Seasons
New Red Fire
Little Gem
Lollo Rossa
Nika
Red Salad Bowl
Saladin

Onion

Allium cepa

Introduction

Onions are amongst the most versatile of vegetables. They are easy to grow and are also very productive – from a relatively small area you can get enough onions to last for many months.

In my opinion, onions are an essential part of any garden and indeed of any dish.

Types of onions

There are two types of bulb onions – spring and autumn types. Either of them can be grown from seed or planted as onion sets. The spring planted crops are generally more reliable, but a few autumn planted sets will extend the harvesting season of onions especially if grown in a polytunnel. Onions have brown, yellow, white, red or purple skins and also come in different shapes.

Soil and site

Onions require a reasonably fertile soil with a good tilth and excellent drainage. If you have a heavy, wet soil it is essential that you make a raised bed to avoid potential disease problems. Spread one bucket of well-decomposed garden compost per square meter. Onions prefer an open, sunny site.

Sowing and planting

Growing from sets:
Growing onions from sets is a lot easier for a beginner. Onion sets are small immature onions. You simply plant the little bulbs between mid-March to mid-April in a well prepared, firm seed bed. Plant red varieties only in mid-April – they are less prone to bolting then.

Autumn onions can be planted in September to early October.

The general recommendation is to plant them so that the top half of the bulb is still showing above ground. In areas where birds like to play with them (or mistake them for some insect) and pull them out, you may need to protect the young sets with a netting for a few weeks.

Onion sets should be firm, rounded, no shoots or roots visible and of small to medium size - the better the sets, the better your crop will be.

Growing from seed:
If you grow onions from seed you have a wonderful choice of varieties, but you need to start the seeds early (late January/February) on a heating bench at 18°C. Onions grown from seed tend to be healthier and less likely to bolt.

I usually sow 4 seeds per cell in a modular tray and place the tray on a heating bench in a greenhouse or polytunnel. Around mid-March I move the tray off the heating bench but still leave it in the tunnel. In early April start hardening off, and in late April they can be planted out. I plant each module containing the 4 seedlings (do not split them up) into the garden.

The following table is for onion sets:

Variety	Sowing	Location	Harvest	Area	Quantity
Troy	15. Sep	Polytunnel	May - June	2m²	80 sets
Sturon	20. Mar	Outdoors	July - Mar	8m²	320 sets
Red Baron	10. Apr	Outdoors	July - Feb	2m²	80 sets

Spacing

Seeds:
Modular grown seedlings (4 seeds per module) are spaced 30cm x 30cm apart each way and staggered.

Sets:
Between rows: 25cm
Between plants: 10cm

Rotation

It is absolutely essential to rotate onions in order to minimise various soil-borne diseases such as white rot.

Plant care

Apart from regular hoeing and weeding, there is little else to do. Be careful, however, that you don't hoe too deep as onions have a very shallow root system.

Harvesting

The overwintered onions in the polytunnel can be used from May onwards as required. You should aim to use them up before the spring planted crop is ready as they do not store well. Spring planted onions are excellent for storing throughout the winter.

Harvest onions in August, when around three quarter of all leaves have turned yellow and fallen over.

The best way to dry the bulbs is to lay them out on the soil not touching each other, in full sun for as long as possible.

Before the weather turns, move the bulbs into an open shed with good air circulation and lay them on chicken wire or pallets in a single layer. Tidy the bulbs and remove any loose skin and soil.

Storing

Once dry, they can be tied in bunches (plaits) and hung in a dry, frost-free shed or even in the kitchen. If properly dried, onions will keep until March the following year.

Important:
Never cut off the stalks of your onions before they have dried otherwise they will rot within a few weeks. If you want to store them loose, wait until the stalks are papery and pull off easily. This is possible about 2 months after pulling.

Self – sufficiency - How much to grow?

It is possible to get onions for 10 to 11 months of the year with just two sowings.

Early summer onions in the polytunnel:
At a spacing of 10cm apart in the row and 4 rows per bed, you'll get 40 onions per m². Thus, 2m² planted in September in a polytunnel will produce 80 onions. You'll get 10 onions per week over a period of 8 weeks from May to June.

Summer onions outdoors for winter storage:
At a spacing of 10cm apart in the row and 4 rows per bed, you'll get 40 onions per m². Thus, 8m² of brown and 2m² of red onions planted in March and April will produce 400 onions. You'll get 10 onions per week over a period of 38 weeks from mid-July to March.

Summary
A total of 12m² produces 480 onions or 10 onions per week for 48 weeks from May to March.

Potential problems

Pests:
Onion fly, onion eelworm and birds.
Diseases:
White rot, neck rot and downy mildew.

Varieties

Centurion
Golden Bear F1
Red Baron
Sturon
Troy (autumn planting)

Oriental Salad

Introduction

There is an ever-increasing range of oriental salads available to the gardener. Most of them are in the brassica family, but there are a few delicious exceptions also mentioned here. It covers salads that don't belong to the lettuce family. Brassica salads tend to be hot and spicy while non-brassica salads have a milder flavour.

Spicy oriental salads complement lettuce – they grow best from autumn to spring when lettuces struggle and do poorly in summer when lettuces thrive.

Soil and site

Any moderately fertile and moisture-retentive soil is suitable, preferably in a sheltered position. It's an ideal crop for a polytunnel throughout the winter months.

Sowing

Oriental salads grow best in the cooler parts of the year. As the days get longer, the plants quickly run to seed. Seeds can be sown directly into a good seedbed or sown into modules (5 seeds per cell) and later transplanted. The plants are quite hardy and can cope with a few degrees of frost. Because plants are quite short-lived, sow in succession of about two to three weeks. In the following sowing plan, the difficult times from late spring to late summer are avoided.
However, with some care you could still get a small crop of these in summer.

<u>Spring salads (mixed varieties) for polytunnel:</u>
Sow in early February and early March in heated propagator (18°C) and plant 4-5 weeks later into polytunnel.

Late summer salads for outdoors:
Sow from mid-June to mid-August and plant out 4 weeks later.
Winter salads for polytunnel:
Sow in mid-September and plant 4 weeks later into polytunnel.

Variety	Sowing	Location	Harvest	Area	Quantity
Various	1. Feb	Polytunnel	April	1m²	16 salads
Various	1. Mar	Polytunnel	May	1m²	16 salads
Various	15. June	Outdoors	August	1m²	16 salads
Various	15. July	Outdoors	September	1m²	16 salads
Various	15. Aug	Outdoors	October	1m²	16 salads
Various	15. Sep	Polytunnel	Oct - Mar	4m²	48 salads

Spacing

Between rows: 25cm
Between plants: 20cm (5 plants per station)

Rotation

The members of the brassica family need to be rotated with the other brassicas.

Plant care

It's important to keep your salads weed free at all times and avoid spilling earth onto the leaves while weeding. During dry spells, you may have to water the plants.

Harvesting

You can either harvest individual leaves as they are needed or use the cut-and-come-again method: cut the whole plant at about 5cm height from the soil level and the leaves will re-grow within the next two to three weeks.

Self – sufficiency - How much to grow?

It is possible to get salads for 10 months of the year from polytunnel and outdoor crops. Late spring and early summer is the most difficult time to grow the brassica members as they are prone to bolting and to fleabeetle attack at this time.

Spring salads - polytunnel crops:
At a spacing of 25cm apart in the row and 4 rows per bed, you'll get 16 salads per m².
Thus, 1m² sown in February and again 1m² sown in early March will yield around 300g per m² per week over a period of 8 weeks from May to June (2.4kg).

Late summer salads outdoors:
At a spacing of 25cm apart in the row and 4 rows per bed, you'll get 16 salads per m².

Thus 1m² sown in mid-June and repeated monthly in mid-July and mid-August will yield around 300g per m² per week over a period of 12 weeks from August to October (3.6kg).

Winter salads – polytunnel crop:
At a spacing of 25cm apart in the row and 4 rows per bed, you'll get 16 salads per m². Thus, 4m² sown in mid September will yield 200g per m² per week over a period of 20 weeks from late October to late March (4kg).

Summary
A total of 9m² produces about 10kg of salad leaves over a period of 9-10 months or 2 salad bags per week. This is a rough guideline only and highly variable between types and season.

Potential problems

Fleabeetles are the worst enemy of the oriental brassica salads but they do not affect the non-brassica salads. They are tiny jumping beetles which eat hundreds of little round holes into the leaves especially in late spring/early summer.
The non-brassica salads are healthy plants with no crop-specific problems.

Varieties

Brassica salads:
Mibuna, Mizuna, Mustard 'Red Frills' and Green Frills, Mustard 'Green in the Snow', Komatsuna, Texel Greens, Pak Choi 'Joi Choi F1', Salad Rocket, Wild Rocket, Tatsoi

Non brassica salads:
Corn salad, Claytonia (Winter Purslane), Summer Purslane, Amaranth Greens, Leaf Beets

Parsnip

(Pastinaca sativa)

Introduction

Parsnip is one of the best crops for the self-sufficient garden. I am delighted that parsnip is still such a popular vegetable in Ireland. In many other countries, it is only grown as an animal feed. From just one sowing you can get a seven month's supply of delicious and nutritious roots.

Site and soil

Parsnips prefer an open, sunny site. Deep sandy soils are ideal but even in heavy soils excellent results can be achieved.
Parsnips prefer well-decomposed compost.

Sowing

The best time to sow parsnips is in late April/early May. Sow seeds directly into the ground about 5cm apart.

Never use modular trays as the tap root will become air-pruned and will start to spiral round itself.
Parsnip seeds are quite big so they can easily be spaced out accurately. They are, however, very papery and light, so choose a calm day for sowing. As soon as the seedlings have germinated you can start thinning them out.

Spacing

The final spacing will determine the size of the root: 10cm spacing produces small roots, 15cm spacing produces medium sized roots and 20cm spacing produces large roots. Spacing between rows is 25cm.
If you forget to thin the seedlings, the parsnips will be no bigger than a pencil.

Rotation

Parsnips should be rotated with the other members of the Umbellifer family.

Plant care

There is very little maintenance apart from thinning and weeding the crop.

Harvesting and storing

Parsnips are ready from October onwards. They are best left in the ground and harvested fresh as required. Parsnips get a better flavour if they are exposed to frost. This changes the stored starch into sugar and makes them sweeter.

If, however, your soil becomes waterlogged it is better to dig them all out and store them in boxes of sand or soil in a cool, frost free shed. They will keep until the following April.

Self – sufficiency - How much to grow?

If you eat 5 parsnip roots per week (Season: October until early April - 25 weeks), you will need 125 parsnip plants.
At a spacing of 20cm apart in the row and 4 rows per bed, you'll get 20 parsnips per m².

Summary
A total of 6m² will produce 125 parsnip roots or 5 parsnip roots per week for 6 months.

Potential problems

Parsnip canker:
Canker is a very common problem with parsnips. I think you will always get a little bit. The symptoms are orange brown spots starting at the shoulder of the root. The variety Javelin F1 has some resistance.

Carrot root fly:
It can affect parsnips as well, but generally to a lesser extent than carrots are affected.

Varieties

Javelin F1
Gladiator F1

Pea

Pisum sativum

Introduction

Peas can be quite prolific but, if neglected, and not harvested regularly, the plants stop producing quickly.

Peas occupy a relatively large area and produce much less compared to most other crops, but if you try to get your children interested in vegetable growing, this is the crop to grow. The yield of peas is difficult to quantify and thus it is difficult to calculate how much you need to grow for self-sufficiency.

Types of peas

There are three types of peas:
- Garden pea (or podding pea)
- Mangetout pea
- Sugar snap pea

The garden pea is the traditional pea, the one you take the seeds out of the pod.

Mangetout types are eaten whole when the pods are still flat. The shells are usually quite thin.

The sugar snap peas are also eaten whole when the pods have swollen (like a normal garden pea) and the shells are usually quite fleshy.

Soil and site

Peas require a sunny and sheltered site. They grow best in a fertile and free-draining soil.

Sowing

Make sure you know what type you are growing (garden pea, sugar snap or mangetout), and label the rows clearly. Otherwise they are easily confused and you do not know at which stage to harvest them.

I always sow peas directly outdoors in drills 4cm deep and 10cm wide.

Seeds are sown 5cm apart in the drill. You can grow them in a single drill in the middle of the bed and support them with a fence, or in a double row 70cm apart and erect a bamboo/branches framework.

Spring peas in polytunnel:
Sow in mid/late February in polytunnel.
Early summer peas outdoors:
Sow mid April directly outdoors.
Late summer peas outdoors:
Sow in early June directly outdoors.

Variety	Sowing	Location	Harvest	Area	Quantity
various	15. Feb	Polytunnel	May - June	2m²	80 seeds
various	15. Apr	Outdoors	June - Aug	4m²	160 seeds
various	1. June	Outdoors	Aug - Sep	4m²	160 seeds

Spacing

Between plants: 5cm
Between rows: 70cm (if you have
a double row)

Rotation

Peas are in the legume family and
should be rotated along with
them.

Plant care

Dwarf peas need little climbing
support. If they are grown in
closely spaced double rows, they
may hold each other up. Any
stragglers could be helped with a
short branch.

Tall pea varieties need to be
trained up adequately. This can
be done with sticks, chicken or
sheep fence or bamboo canes.
Peas, however, find it difficult to
climb up bamboo canes, so you
should use twigs in between the
canes. Remember to check the
height of the variety you grow
and erect a high enough frame
for the peas.

Harvesting

Peas can be harvested from May
(Polytunnel) until September. The
pods should be picked regularly
(once or twice a week). If you do
not harvest regularly and allow the
plants to ripen their seeds, they will
soon stop flowering.

Storing

Peas are best eaten fresh. If you
have too many, you can blanch and
freeze them for the winter months.

Self-sufficiency -
How much to grow?

Peas take up a lot of space, but are
very important due to their
nitrogen fixing capacity and for
providing high protein food. The
highest yielding type is the sugar
snap pea. A rough guideline is
$1kg/m^2$ of podded garden peas,
$1kg/m^2$ of mangetout peas and
$1.5kg/m^2$ of sugar snap peas.

Early spring polytunnel crop:
At a spacing of 5cm apart in the
row and 2 rows per bed, you'll need
to sow 40 seeds per m^2. $1m^2$ of
peas will yield about 1kg of shelled
peas.

Thus, 2m² sown in mid February will produce 2kg of actual peas from May to June.

Spring sown crop outdoors:
At a spacing of 5cm apart in the row and 2 rows per bed, you'll need to sow 40 seeds per m². 1m² of peas will yield about 1kg of shelled peas. Thus, 4m² sown in mid-April will produce 4kg of actual peas from June to July.

Early summer sown crop outdoors:
At a spacing of 5cm apart in the row and 2 rows per bed, you'll need to sow 40 seeds per m². 1m² of peas will yield about 1kg of shelled peas. Thus, 4m² sown in early June will produce 4kg of actual peas from August to September.

Summary
A total of 10m² produces 10kg of peas (actual beans). If you blanch and freeze them in 200g bags, you'll get a 50 weeks supply of peas.
This can be a mixture of the different types of peas.

Potential problems

Mice can be a problem, especially when they find the newly-planted delicious seeds. The main disease problem is powdery mildew.

Varieties

Garden Peas:
Hurst Greenshaft

Mangetout:
Carouby de Maussane (very tall, purple flowers)
Delikata
Oregon Sugar Pod
Dwarf Sweet Green (dwarf type)
Shiraz (purple podded)

Sugar Snap:
Sugar Ann
Sugar Snap

Peppers & Chillies

Capsicum frutescens annuum

Introduction

Peppers and chilli peppers can only be grown in a polytunnel or greenhouse. In my opinion, peppers take as much space as a tomato plant and only yield a dozen peppers per plant. Chilli peppers, on the other hand, can produce over 100 chillies and are ideal for the productive self-sufficient garden. A few pepper plants for the occasional treat are essential.

The Scoville test rates the heat of chillies on a scale of zero to over a million Scoville Heat Units (SHU). The world's hottest chilli variety keeps changing as there is a constant race for yet another record.

Soil and site

Peppers and chilli peppers prefer a rich, loamy soil with plenty of well-rotted compost added to it. They need to grow in full sun, so ensure that there is no shading from other crops.

Sowing

Chilli peppers and peppers require a long growing season and should be sown as early as February. I usually sow the seeds in a small standard seed tray or pot and space the seeds 2cm apart from each other covered with 1cm compost. The tray should be placed into a warm propagator (20-23°C) or warm windowsill. The seedlings start to appear two weeks after sowing.

About ten days after they have germinated, they should be pricked out into 7 cm pots using potting compost. Three or four weeks later, they can be potted on into a 10cm pot.

Planting

Chilli peppers and peppers dislike cold temperatures, they can only be planted into the greenhouse or tunnel in early May in mild areas or in mid to late May in cooler districts.

Spacing

Between plants: 45cm
Between rows: 45cm

Plant care

Apart from regular watering, there is little else you need to do. If the plants grow too upright, you can pinch out the growing shoot at about 30cm height. This encourages the plants to become bushier. Depending on the variety, this may not be necessary as some branch out naturally. The plants may require a single stake to prevent them from falling over.

Harvesting and storing

Harvest chillies and peppers throughout the summer whenever required. All fruits start off green and then turn into their final colour. Towards the end of the growing season in October I usually harvest all the remaining chillies and dry them in the kitchen. They can be made into necklaces that can be hung in the kitchen.

Self – sufficiency - How much to grow?

Sweet peppers:
From each pepper plant, you'll get about 10 peppers per plant over a period of 3 months from July to September.
At a spacing of 4 plants per m^2, you'll get 40 peppers per m^2.
From a sowing of $3m^2$ in February and planted in May, you'll get 120 peppers from July to September.

Summary
A total of $3m^2$ (12 plants) will produce around 120 peppers or 10 peppers per week for 3 months.

Chilli peppers:
From each pepper plant, you'll get about 80 chilli peppers per plant over a period of 4 months from July to October.
At a spacing of 4 plants/m^2, you'll get 320 chillies per m^2.

From a sowing of 2m² in February and planted in May, you'll get 640 chilli peppers from July to October. Chilli peppers can be dried and will last until the following crop is ready next July.

Summary
A total of 2m² (8 plants) will produce around 640 chilli peppers or 12 chilli peppers every week throughout the whole year.

Potential problems

Chilli peppers are very prone to aphid attacks. Both whitefly and greenfly feed on the leaves of the plants. A regular application of a garlic spray before the problem arises can provide an effective control. If aphids are already present, a biological control can be used.

Varieties

Sweet Peppers:
Bell Boy F1
Roberta F1
Teseo (large elongated shape – delicious, reliable and great yield)

Chilli Peppers:
Hungarian Hot Wax
Prairie Fire
Ring of Fire

Potato

Solanum tuberosum

Introduction

Potatoes are still the staple crop in many countries, especially in Ireland. They are easy to grow and, if you can avoid blight, a good harvest is guaranteed. Potatoes are an excellent first crop to get your garden started.

Types of potatoes

Potatoes are classified according to their time of maturity:
- First early
- Second early
- Maincrop

The early varieties mature much quicker than maincrop potatoes. In most years, they are also able to avoid blight as they are harvested before blight arrives. Maincrop potatoes produce a higher yield and can be stored over winter. Second early potatoes are in between.

There are hundreds of varieties available. They come in various shapes (round, oval, knobbly), sizes, colours (red, white, blue, purple and the flesh white, yellow, mottled or blue) and textures (waxy or floury).

Soil and site

Potatoes prefer an open, sunny and frost-free site. The soil should be fertile and free-draining. Avoid low-lying frost pockets. They require a generous application of well-decomposed compost or manure.

Planting

Potatoes can either be planted in ridges (single row) or using a bed system (double row). If they are planted in ridges, it is much easier to earth them up.

Plant the seed tubers 10 to 15cm deep. Early potatoes for the polytunnel can be chitted in order to get an earlier crop.

Chitting:
Buy your early seed potatoes in late December/early January and place them in shallow trays in a light frost-free room. Once the sturdy green shoots appear you can plant the tubers in the polytunnel.

Planting times:

First early potatoes in polytunnel:
Plant chitted tubers in late January directly into polytunnel beds or drill (Varieties: Red Duke of York, Sharpes Express, Homeguard).

Second early potatoes in polytunnel:
Plant chitted tubers in early March directly into polytunnel beds or drill (Variety: Orla).

Early potatoes outdoors:
Plant chitted (or non-chitted) tubers in mid-March directly into drills outdoors (Variety: Orla).

Maincrop potatoes outdoors:
Plant tubers in mid-April directly into drills outdoors (Varieties: Carolus, Seville, Sarpo Mira, Cara).

Variety	Sowing	Location	Harvest	Area	Qty
Duke of York	25. Jan	Polytunnel	May - June	4m²	32 tubers
Orla	1. Mar	Polytunnel	June - July	4m²	32 tubers
Orla	15. Mar	Outdoors	July - Sep	8m²	64 tubers
Sarpo Mira	15. Apr	Outdoors	Oct - Apr	8m²	48 tubers
Carolus	15. Apr	Outdoors	Oct - Apr	8m²	48 tubers

Spacing

Early potatoes:
Between plants: 25cm
Between rows: 50cm
Maincrop potatoes:
Between plants: 35cm
Between rows: 75cm

Rotation

Potatoes are susceptible to a wide range of diseases. Thus, it is essential that they follow a strict rotation programme.

Plant care

In case there is a danger of frost and your potato shoots are just appearing you can protect them by earthing them up and covering the shoots with soil for protection.
Alternatively, you can cover the plants with a frost protection fleece.
When the haulm (shoot) is about 20cm high you should earth them up again. Use a draw hoe and pull loose soil against the haulm. Cover roughly half of the stem (10cm). When the leaves have become blighted, you can cut off the stalks and dispose of them.

Harvesting and storing

Early potatoes can be harvested whenever you feel they are big enough to use. Some books recommend waiting until they form flowers, but this is very dependent on the variety you grow.
With early potatoes never dig more than you need at a time as the tubers will not store well.
Maincrop potatoes should be left in the ground until October even if you had to cut the stalks off for blight control much earlier. If stored in boxes of sand or soil in a cool, frost-free shed, they will keep until April of the following year.

Self – sufficiency - How much to grow?

To produce enough potatoes to feed your family throughout the year is very satisfying.

First early polytunnel crops:
It is possible to get around 4kg of potatoes per m². A little less early on but then tuber yield increases daily.

Thus, 4m² planted in late January and again 4m² planted in early March will produce 32kg of early potatoes or 3.2kg of potatoes per week over a period of 10 weeks from May to mid-July.

Early potatoes outdoors:
Yield: 5kg of potatoes per m². Thus, 8m² planted in mid-March will produce 40kg of potatoes or 4kg of potatoes per week over a period of 10 weeks from mid-July to late September.

Maincrop potatoes outdoors:
Yield: 6kg of potatoes per m². Thus, 16m² planted in mid-March will produce 96kg of potatoes or 3.8kg of potatoes per week over a period of 25 weeks from October to March.

Summary
A total of 32m² produces 168kg of potatoes or around 3.5kg of potatoes per week for 11 months.

Potential problems
The list of potential potato troubles is endless. The most common ones are frost damage (when plants emerge in late spring), blight (July – August), scab (quite harmless if not too severe) and slugs (late summer/ early autumn).

In a damp climate, slugs can be the most devastating problem with potatoes. One year, I lost my entire crop. Slugs burrowed into the tubers and ate them from the inside out. Luckily, you can spot the damage early on. These slugs come out at night and eat the leaves of the potatoes, so as soon as you see the first symptoms of nibbled leaves, spread organic slug pellets around the plants and repeat a couple of weeks later.

Varieties

Early potatoes:
Colleen
Homeguard
Orla
Red Duke of York
Sharpes Express

Maincrop potatoes:
Cara
Carolus
Nicola
Pink Fir Apple
Sarpo Mira
Sevilla
Vitabella

Scallions or spring onions

Allium cepa

Introduction

Scallions are a very popular salad vegetable. They are grown for their small, white shanks and tender, green stem and leaves. They are very easy and quick to grow, but in order to get a continuous supply you need to make regular sowings.

Soil and site

Scallions require the same soil and site condition as onions.

Sowing

Sow 10 seeds per cell in modular trays and place on a propagator (18°C) for early sowings. When planting out the ten seedlings, do not separate them, but plant them together in a bunch.
The advantage of this is that you can easily hoe between the bunches and they are very easy to harvest whole. Seedlings take about 4 weeks from sowing to planting out and then a further 6 weeks to harvesting. The variety Ishikura Bunching lasts well in the garden for at least 4 weeks once they are ready.

Sowing times:

First early scallions in polytunnel:
Sow 10 seeds/cell in modular trays on heating bench (18°C) in early February and again in early March. Plant into polytunnel four 4 after sowing.

Summer scallions outdoors:
Sow 10 seeds/cell in modular trays in early April, mid-May and again in early July. Plant outdoors 4 weeks after sowing.

Autumn scallions in polytunnel:
Sow 10 seeds/cell in modular trays in early August and early September. Plant into polytunnel 4 weeks after sowing.

Variety	Sowing	Location	Harvest	Area	Quantity
Ishikura	1. Feb	Polytunnel	May	0.5m²	8 bunches
Ishikura	1. Mar	Polytunnel	June	0.5m²	8 bunches
Ishikura	1. Apr	Outdoors	July	0.5m²	8 bunches
Ishikura	15. May	Outdoors	Aug	0.5m²	8 bunches
Ishikura	1. July	Outdoors	Sep	0.5m²	8 bunches
Ishikura	1. Aug	Polytunnel	Oct	0.5m²	8 bunches
Ishikura	1. Sep	Polytunnel	Nov	0.5m²	8 bunches

Spacing

Plant bunches of ten seedlings together at a spacing of 25 x 25cm which gives 16 bunches of scallions per m².

Rotation

It is important to keep scallions in the allium section in your garden to minimise various soil-borne diseases.

Plant care

Scallions prefer to grow on moist soil. If it is too dry, they may develop a bulbous growth and watering may be necessary.

Harvesting

Scallions are ready about 9 to 10 weeks after sowing. Harvesting is very easy if they are already growing in bunches. Harvest a bunch at a time as required.

Self – sufficiency - How much to grow?

With 7 sowing dates and only half a meter of a bed per sowing, you'll get all the scallions you need for 7 months.

Early scallions polytunnel crop:
At a spacing of 25cm apart in the row and 4 rows per bed, you'll get 16 scallions per m². Thus, 0.5m² sown in early February and again in early March will produce 16 bunches of scallions (each containing 10 scallions) or 2 bunches of scallions per week over a period of 8 weeks from May to June.

Summer scallions outdoors:
At a spacing of 25cm apart in the row and 4 rows per bed, you'll get 16 scallions per m². Thus, 0.5m² sown in early April, mid-May and again in early July will produce 24 bunches of scallions (each containing 10 scallions) or 2 bunches of scallions per week over a period of 12 weeks from July to September.

Autumn scallions polytunnel crop:
At a spacing of 25cm apart in the row and 4 rows per bed, you'll get 16 scallions per m². Thus, 0.5m² sown in early August and again in early September will produce 16 bunches of scallions or 2 bunches of scallions per week over a period of 8 weeks from October to November.

Summary
A total of 3.5m² produces 56 bunches (560 scallions) or 2 bunches per week for 7 months.

Potential problems

Scallions may suffer from the same pests and diseases as onions, but to a much lesser extent because they mature much faster. Downy mildew is the only problem I have encountered with scallions, and only if I left the plants too long in the ground.

Varieties

Ishikura Bunching
Parade

Spinach, Perpetual and Chard

Beta vulgaris subsp. *flavescens*

Introduction

Perpetual spinach, Swiss chard, ruby and rainbow chard are by far the best value crop in the garden. From a very small area and a few sowings, you can get healthy greens for most of the year. Perpetual spinach and the various chards have the same growing conditions and will be treated as one in this self-sufficient guide. You can grow a mixture of one of the above or just a single one. The most under-rated and under-used type is, in my opinion, Swiss chard. The leaf stems (petioles) make a delicious vegetable that can be stir-fried as well as the dark green leaves which can be used like spinach.

Soil and site

Perpetual spinach and chard will do well in any fertile soil but it is a greedy plant. The more compost or composted manure you give it, the higher the plants will yield.

Sowing and planting

Perpetual spinach and chard can be raised in modular trays placed on a bench in a greenhouse (or tunnel). Sow one seed per module about 1.5cm deep. They usually germinate within 6 to 7 days (at 18°C). You will notice that from the one seed about 3-5 seedlings appear. They are clusters of seeds. In order to get a good strong plant, I recommend thinning out the seedlings to leave just the strongest one in each cell. Seedlings are ready for planting out about 4 weeks after sowing.

Early spring polytunnel crop:
Sow in late January in heated propagator (at 18°C) and plant in early March in polytunnel.
Summer/autumn crop outdoors:
Sow in early April in a heated propagator (at 18°C) and plant in early May outdoors.
Autumn/winter crop outdoors:
Sow in mid-May and plant outdoors.
Winter/spring polytunnel crop:
Sow in early September and plant in polytunnel.

Variety	Sowing	Location	Harvest	Area	Quantity
Mix	31. Jan	Polytunnel	Mar - May	1m²	9 plants
Mix	1. April	Outdoors	June - Sep	2m²	18 plants
Mix	25. May	Outdoors	Aug - Nov	2m²	18 plants
Mix	1. Sep	Polytunnel	Nov - Mar	3m²	27 plants

Spacing

Between plants: 30cm
Between rows: 30cm

Rotation

Perpetual spinach and chard are not susceptible to any specific pests and diseases. They can be grown in any part of the rotation.

Plant care

It's really such an easy vegetable to grow. All you need to do is keep the crop weed free and well watered during dry spells. It's also beneficial to remove the lower leaves which turn brown if not harvested on time.

Harvesting

Harvest leaves throughout the growing season by twisting them away from the base of the plant. It is a down, twist movement. Try it a few times to get practice. It is much better for the plant than cutting it and ending up with diseased little stumps.

Self-sufficiency - How much to grow?

If you eat spinach and chard regularly – one square metre or 9 plants per sowing are sufficient.

Early spring polytunnel crop:
At a spacing of 30cm apart in the row and 3 rows per bed, you'll get 9 perpetual spinach/chard plants per m². Thus, 1m² sown in late January, will produce a minimum of 0.5kg of spinach/chard leaves per week over a period of 8 weeks from late March to late May (4kg).

Summer outdoor crop:
At a spacing of 30cm apart in the row and 3 rows per bed, you'll get 9 perpetual spinach/chard plants per m².

Thus, 2m² sown in early April will produce a minimum of 0.5kg of spinach/chard leaves per week over a period of 16 weeks from June to September (8kg).

Winter/spring outdoor crop:
At a spacing of 30cm apart in the row and 3 rows per bed you'll get 9 perpetual spinach/chard plants per m². Thus, 2m² sown in May, will produce 0.5kg of spinach/chard leaves per week over a period of 16 weeks from August to November (8kg).

Winter/spring crop in polytunnel:
At a spacing of 30cm apart in the row and 3 rows per bed, you'll get 9 perpetual spinach/chard plants per m². Thus, 3m² sown in early September, will produce 0.5kg of spinach/chard leaves per week over a period of 20 weeks from November to March (10kg).

Summary
A total of 8m² produces over 0.5kg of perpetual spinach/chard leaves per week for 12 months of the year.

Varieties

Perpetual spinach
Rainbow chard
Ruby chard
Swiss chard

Squash & Pumpkin

Cucurbita maxima, pepo and *moschata*

Introduction

Squashes and pumpkins are one of the most vigorous vegetables and are only suitable for the self-sufficient garden if you have plenty of space available. They are handy plants to cover a large area but, if growing space is in short supply, you may grow less of them.

Types:

- Summer squashes
- Winter squashes and pumpkins

For both types there are bush and trailing varieties. The bush plants are a lot better behaved and require a lot less space than the trailing varieties but the yield is lower.

Summer squashes are grown and harvested like courgettes. There are only a few varieties available but some of them are excellent.

Winter squashes are grown for storage. The fruit is harvested in October before the first frost and stored. There is a huge choice of varieties available. Immature fruits of winter squash can also be used throughout the season.

Soil and site

Squashes need a very fertile, free-draining soil which can hold plenty of moisture.

A generous application of well-decomposed compost is beneficial (about one bucket per square metre). They also need a sheltered place in the garden.

Sowing

Squashes are very tender plants. I usually sow seeds in early May, individually into 7cm pots. Ideally, the pots are left in a propagator in the greenhouse or on the window-sill at home (south-facing).

After about 3 weeks, or before the plants get pot bound, I pot them on into 12cm pots which are still left in the greenhouse or indoors.

Variety	Sowing	Location	Harvest	Area	Quantity
Various	1. May	Outdoors	October	9m²	5 plants

Planting

Start hardening the plants off towards the end of May and plant out in early June. Do not plant if the weather forecast predicts cold windy spells which are quite common during this time. The safest way would be to plant them under cloches which are covered with bionet.

Spacing

Bush varieties: 1.2m apart each way.
Trailing varieties: 2m apart each way.

Rotation

Squashes and pumpkins belong to the cucurbit family. This family is not prone to any soil-borne pests or diseases so you do not need to be too fussy with rotation.

Plant care

Keep the plants weed-free, especially in the early stages as it will be very difficult later on to get to the weeds. Pumpkins and squashes may try to grow over neighbouring vegetables, so they need to be kept in check, either by shortening some shoots or by moving them back to their allocated space.

Harvesting and storing

Summer squashes should be harvested every week. Some varieties, such as Sunburst F1, are very prolific. If you let the fruits mature, the yield will be reduced. Summer squashes are not included in this self-sufficient guide, but could be added to courgettes.

Winter squashes are harvested in late autumn before the first frost. If you want to store squashes, leave the fruits to mature on the vine at least until October. The mature fruits have hard outer shells. Use a sharp knife to cut the stems (or handles) of the fruits to be stored and leave the stem attached to the fruit. Pumpkins and squashes store well in a dry, fairly cool location until March the following year.

Self – sufficiency - How much to grow?

From each squash/pumpkin plant you will get around 3 decent sized fruits.

Summary
A total of 9m² (5 plants) will produce around 15 squash/pumpkin fruits or one fruit per week.

Tip:
I use squash and pumpkin plants when I get an area ready for the following year. I spread compost or manure onto the grass and then cover with black plastic. This is left for 12 months. I cut a small slit into the plastic and grow squashes and pumpkins through it. Thus, I don't waste important growing space.

Potential problems

Squash plants need to be protected from slugs at the early stages straight after planting out. Like all other cucurbits, they are very sensitive to cold and windy weather. It is highly beneficial to plant them under a cloche covered with bionet for the first month.

Varieties

Summer squash:
Sunburst F1

Winter squash:
Crown Prince F1 (one of the best flavoured squashes, steel grey skin and orange flesh)
Turk's Turban
Uchiki Kuri
Vegetable Spaghetti

Swede & Turnip

Brassica napus

Introduction

Swedes are very closely related to turnips. The name swede is an abbreviation of Swedish turnip. Swedes generally have yellow flesh as opposed to the white flesh of turnips.

Both are good crops for the self-sufficient garden.
They prefer our mild and moist growing conditions and they are also one of the highest yielding vegetables.

Soil and site

Swedes and turnips will grow in a range of soils, provided they are reasonably fertile. Compost application is highly beneficial. Both suffer if there is a boron deficiency in the soil.

Sowing and planting

In theory, swedes and turnips can be sown directly outdoors in drills, but you will get much better results if you raise them in modular trays. You sow one seed in each cell 2cm deep and keep the modular tray in a tunnel or on the windowsill. The seeds will germinate within a week and after about 4 weeks they are ready to be hardened off and can then be planted out.
I would grow turnips early in the year and in summer and keep the swedes for the winter months and for storage.

First early turnip in polytunnel:
Sow in modular trays in late January in heated propagator (18°C) and plant in early March in polytunnel.
Second early turnip in polytunnel:
Sow in modular trays in early March in heated propagator (18°C) and plant in early April in polytunnel.

<u>Summer swede and turnips outdoors:</u>
Sow in modular trays in mid-April and plant in mid-May into outdoor beds.
<u>Maincrop/storage swede outdoors:</u>
Sow in modular trays in late May and plant in late June into outdoor beds.

Variety	Sowing	Location	Harvest	Area	Quantity
Turnip	30. Jan	Polytunnel	Apr- May	1m²	24 roots
Turnip	1. Mar	Polytunnel	May- June	1m²	24 roots
Swede & turnip	15. Apr	Outdoors	July - Sep	3m²	72 roots
Swede	25. May	Outdoors	Oct - Feb	5m²	120 roots

Spacing

<u>Turnips and small swedes:</u>
Between plants: 15cm
Between rows: 25cm

<u>Large swedes:</u>
Between plants: 30cm
Between rows: 25cm
In order to get large Swedes you can harvest every second root when it is of reasonable size.

Rotation

It is absolutely essential to keep them in the brassica section of your rotation to prevent a build up of the numerous brassica pests and diseases.

Plant care

Keep the soil hoed and watered during dry periods. This will prevent the roots from getting tough and woody.

Harvesting and storage

From the early sowing, both turnips and swedes can be harvested as required at whichever size you prefer. Maincrop swedes can either be harvested in October and stored in boxes of sand/soil or you can risk leaving them in the ground. They can easily withstand some frost, but I suggest that if your ground becomes waterlogged in winter you need to store them safely.

Self – sufficiency - How much to grow?

It is possible to get a decent amount of turnip and swede for 11 months of the year from a number of sowings in the polytunnel and outdoors.

Spring turnip - polytunnel crops:
At a spacing of 15cm apart in the row and 4 rows per bed, you'll get 24 turnips per m².

Thus, 1m² sown in late January, and again, 1m² sown in early March, will produce 48 turnips – or 6 turnips per week over a period of 8 weeks from April to May.

Summer turnip and swede oudoors:
At an initial spacing of 15cm apart in the row and 4 rows per bed, you'll get 24 turnips/swedes per m². Thus, 3m² sown in mid-April will produce 72 turnips/swedes, or 6 turnips/swedes per week over a period of 12 weeks from July to mid-September.

Winter maincrop swede outdoors:
At an initial spacing of 15cm apart in the row and 4 rows per bed, you'll get 24 swedes per m². Thus, 5m² sown in late May will produce 120 swedes – or 6 swedes per week over a period of 20 weeks from October to early February.

Summary
A total of 10m² will produce 240 turnips/swedes or 6 roots per week for 40 weeks.

Potential problems

Swedes and turnips are susceptible to all the brassica troubles, particularly the fleabeetle which can decimate young seed leaves.

To minimise this danger, you can raise the seedling in modular trays so they are already more established when planted out. There is also a special fleabeetle netting available.

Varieties

Swedes:
Helenor
Gowrie
Marian

Turnips:
Milan Purple Top
Oasis
Snowball
White Globe

Tomato

Lycopersicon esculentum

Introduction

Tomatoes are certainly one of the most exciting tunnel and green-house vegetables and a must for a self-sufficient garden.

The flavour of home-grown tomatoes can never be matched by the bland and thick-skinned supermarket tomatoes.

Soil and site

Tomatoes require a very fertile soil enriched with composted farmyard manure or garden compost. I usually incorporate a full wheelbarrow of composted manure into the soil for every three square metres.

Sowing

Tomatoes need to be raised on a heating bench (21°C) or warm south-facing windowsill.

Seeds are best sown from mid-February until mid-March into traditional open seed trays (not modular trays). Seeds should be sown thinly into the trays (about 100 seeds per standard tray) or pots (about 10 seeds per 9cm pot). Then, the seeds should be covered lightly with seed compost using a sieve and pressed in using a wooden board that fits snugly into the tray.

Keep the trays moist at all times – never overwater them or let them dry out. The tomato seedlings should emerge after 10 days. It is very important to prick out the seedlings as early as possible, ideally into 10cm pots containing potting compost. Remember to hold the seedling on the seed leaves (cotyledons) and plant the seedling so the seed leaves are just above soil level. During this stage, the plants should remain on the heating bench.

Young plants in pots must be spaced out as soon as their leaves are touching – roughly about every three weeks. If you fail to do this, the plants will become weak and spindly.

Variety	Sowing	Location	Harvest	Area	Quantity
Cherry types	20. Feb	Polytunnel	July- Oct	3m²	12 plants
Beefsteak types	20. Feb	Polytunnel	Aug- Oct	1m²	4 plants
Standard types	20. Feb	Polytunnel	July– Oct	1m²	4 plants

Planting

Tomatoes can be planted in May and trained up strings that are attached to an overhead wire. After digging the planting hole, lay the bottom part of the string into the hole and the other end tied to the overhead wire. Plant the tomato plant on top of the string and cover and gently firm the soil around the plant to leave no air pocket around the plant. If your tomato plants have become leggy, you can plant them deeper. This will strengthen the plants.

Spacing

The plants should be spaced out 50cm apart. You can have a single or double row per bed. The yield is higher from a double row, but a single row usually produces healthier plants. For a double row, you need 4 plants/m².

Plant care

Every week you will have to side-shoot your tomato plants. Many beginners find it difficult to distinguish between a leaf, a side-shoot and a fruiting truss. The side-shoot is always the one in the middle – the one between the main stem and the leaf.

The fruiting truss can be recognised by small yellow flowers and there is never a leaf below. Never remove the fruiting trusses otherwise you'll have no tomatoes.

No matter how long the side shoots are, even if they already have flowers or fruit on them, you have to remove them. When they are still quite small, you can easily nip them off with your fingers. When they are bigger you need to use a sharp knife or secateurs.

Side-shooting tomatoes

Apart from regular side-shooting, you should also wind the growing plant around the twine, or tie onto canes if that is your training method. The lower leaves of the plants should be removed as soon as they start to discolour.

Bush or Cordon Types

There are two different growth habits of tomatoes. The first group consists of the tall tomatoes. Seed catalogues often describe them as indeterminate or cordon types. These are the ones you will have to side-shoot and train up strings or canes. The second group are the dwarf or bush tomatoes. They are suitable for growing in pots or hanging baskets. Bush tomatoes do not need to be side-shooted. They will only grow to about 50cm in height and can be left to their own devices.

Harvesting

You can expect your first harvest of tomatoes in July, possibly slightly earlier in warmer parts of the country. My favourite variety, 'Sungold F1', is always the first one to ripen, and often the one that lasts longest. It is also high yielding – sometimes producing up to 400 cherry tomatoes per plant. Overall, the average yield of tomatoes, if well grown, is 2 to 3 kg/plant.

Self – sufficiency - How much to grow?

From each tomato plant you will get about 2.5kg of tomatoes during its growing period. The harvesting season is from early July to late October – 18 weeks.

From 5m² (20 plants), you'll get 50kg of tomatoes.

Over 18 weeks, you'll get 2.7kg of tomatoes per week from early July to late October.

Summary
A total of 5m² (20 plants) will produce around 50kg of tomatoes or 2.7kg tomatoes per week for 18 weeks.

Any excess tomatoes can easily be frozen and used for the winter months for soups and other dishes.

Potential problems

Unfortunately, tomatoes can be affected by a whole range of pests, diseases and disorders. There are too many to list – so please refer to my other book: "Fruit & Vegetables for the Polytunnel and Greenhouse."

Varieties

Iris (beef)
Pantano Romanesco (beef)
Rosella (cherry)
Sakura F1 (cherry)
Shirley F1 (standard)
Sungold F1 (cherry)
Sweet Aperitif (cherry)
Tigerella (striped standard)

Yacon

Polymnia sonchifolia or *Smallanthus sonchifolia*

Introduction

Yacon is one of my favourite vegetables to grow. It originates in the Andes and was one of the Inca vegetables. It produces large edible tubers. In a tunnel or greenhouse it can grow into a large plant and produces a very high yield of sweet tasting tubers that can be eaten raw or cooked. It is very likely to become one of the new superfoods due to its health-promoting, high fructo-oligosaccharide content.

It has been made into a syrup sweetener that is both healthy and with low calories. It is included in the self-sufficiency book because of its very high yield in tubers, but also because I travelled to Peru and New Zealand to study this plant.

Soil and site

Yacon requires a free-draining, fertile and well-balanced soil and should be grown in full sun. In cooler parts of the country, it does best in a polytunnel where it lends a tropical appearance. In more favourable areas, it grows well outdoors.

Sowing and planting

Yacon can only be grown from stem tubers. The problem is that they are so difficult to get hold of. Yacon plants have two types of tubers – very knobbly ones that cluster around the stalk and beautiful, large, smooth and succulent tubers that grow outside of the knobbly ones. The smooth succulent ones are for eating, and the knobbly ones for propagation. The knobbly tubers can be separated in late March/early April and, provided that they have a growth point, will make a new plant. Each part should be potted on into a 1 or 2 litre pot depending on the size of the tuber using good potting compost. The pots should be placed on the heating bench or a south-facing window sill in the house. The plants can be planted into the tunnel or greenhouse around late April or outdoors in late May.

I recommend starting off with just one plant in the corner of a polytunnel and one plant outdoors. You can then propagate the plant to get more in the following years.

Spacing

The plants grow huge with a spread similar to a courgette plant and a height of about 1.5 to 2 metres.
Between plants: 1 metre

Plant care

Apart from regular watering, there is no need for additional maintenance.

Harvesting and storing

You should leave the plants in the ground until the first frost has killed the leaves. The tubers seem to grow a lot during the end of the season so the later the first frost, the higher the yield. The yield of tubers can be truly phenomenal and no other crop can match it. In one year, I got a yield of nearly 20kg from one plant.
Carefully dig out the whole plant and remove the smooth succulent tubers and use them immediately or store them in moist sand in a frost-free shed. What is left is the knobbly part of the plant. Store that in a bucket of moist sand in a frost-free shed. This can be split up the following spring and you can give some new plants to your friends.

Uses

The tubers are best eaten raw like a fruit. When eaten raw, they have a surprisingly sweet taste. When cooked, they remain crunchy and can be used as a potato alternative. They are delicious roasted.

Potential problems

One of the advantages of 'new' vegetables is that they are often free of any specific pests and diseases. Apart from an occasional slug nibble on the leaves, they grow completely healthy.

Varieties
There are a number of yacon varieties but they are difficult to get.

Self-sufficient Ireland

While I was preparing various cropping plans for a self-sufficient garden, I thought it would be a good idea to find out how self-sufficient Ireland is in food production.

One would imagine with a low population density and so much farmland, we would be a major exporter of fresh vegetables. Unfortunately, this is not the case and a missed opportunity. The good thing is the land is there and, with a few changes in policy, this could quickly be changed so that Ireland would be self-sufficient in vegetables, fruit and cereals.

In my opinion, every country should make it a priority to be able to provide sufficient food for its citizens.
In fact, this should be the number one priority, alongside clean water and air.

Here are some calculations:
Ireland has 6.9 million hectares of land, 4.4 million hectares are used for agriculture and 0.73 million hectares for forestry. Of the agricultural land area, 80% is pasture, 12% rough grazing, 8% is crops (cereals, fruit and vegetables). Cereals account for 272,200 hectares, potatoes 9,100 hectares and vegetables account for 4,500 hectares (DAFM statistics 2016).

Carrots and cabbage are the most important crops in terms of land area with carrots accounting for 800 hectares and cabbage 650 hectares.
Let's presume we only use one twentieth of the agricultural land area (4,400,000 hectares) for vegetable production. This equates to 220,000 hectares. Based on the presumption that 1ha will provide sufficient vegetables for 25 families or 100 people - 220,000ha would feed 22 million people.

Therefore, only one twentieth of the currently used agriculture land area would provide sufficient food for 22 million people, and this doesn't even take into account the actual garden areas where people grow their own food.

In order to provide vegetables for 5 million people, we would only need 50,000 hectares. Currently we only have 13,600 hectares under potatoes and vegetables. We have a potential, or responsibility, to nearly quadruple the land area for vegetable production. In other words, we currently only produce vegetables for just over 1 million people.

Let's take carrots as an example: We produce 800 hectares of carrots in Ireland, with an average yield of 65 t/ha. That's a total of 52,000 tonnes or 52,00,000kg. With a population of close to 5 million people, we can each get 10.4kg of carrots per person per year. I would eat this in a month!

What I wanted to cover is that there is a lot of potential to grow your own food as well as planning to set up a market garden. We are nowhere near self-sufficiency in vegetables in Ireland, and if there ever is a crisis in logistics or drought or floods in different countries, we are not in a good position at the far edge of Europe.

On a positive note, vegetable production in Ireland has many advantages over many other countries. There is still plenty of land and water available, especially if we mind it well.

Worldwide, access to water has already become one of the main limiting factors for food production. This puts Ireland in a very important position for the future and we may well change from an importer of vegetables to becoming a supplier to many countries where food production will become more difficult in a changing climate.

Growing fruit

There can't be a self-sufficient garden without growing fruit. It would nearly deserve a full book in itself. Unfortunately, I have to limit myself to just the main points. My favourite fruit growing book is by Ben Pike: "The Fruit Tree Handbook".

Growing apples

Apples are by far the easiest and most popular fruit tree. They can also be trained to suit any size garden. An apple espalier would make a beautiful and productive edging for your vegetable plot. Alternatively, if you have more space you can grow an apple orchard. There are numerous rootstocks available – these determine the size of the apple tree. Always choose the correct rootstock for your type of garden.

For an espalier or small garden, choose an M27 or M9 rootstock or, for larger gardens, choose an M26 or MM106, M111 or M25.

I often think an apple tree is the best investment. A tree may cost between €12 and €20, and 2 to 3 years later you'll get at least 50 apples per tree. In the fifth year you can expect at least 200 apples per tree.

With little maintenance, you'll get a good crop most years for around 15 years for the smaller rootstocks, 25 years for the medium-sized rootstocks and 80 years for the large orchard types. Organic apples cost around 50c each. With 200 apples per year, you'll save/earn €100 on apples on a once-off investment of €12. I know that's not, and should not be, the reason for growing your own apples. It's fun, easy, and home-grown unsprayed apples are one of the healthiest foods around.

I'm often disappointed by shop-bought apples, even the organic ones.

There are only a few varieties available and mostly with a bland, overly sweet taste. Get ready for an explosion of taste and texture which you'll only get when you eat an apple directly from the tree.

Apple varieties

There are hundreds, if not thousands of apple varieties available, with well over 100 native Irish varieties.

It is very important to choose a good variety of apple. I always advice not to buy the varieties you know the name of – Gala, Cox Orange Pippin, Pink Lady, or Golden Delicious – these are not suitable for our climate conditions and are very prone to scab and canker.

My favourite varieties are Charles Ross, James Grieve, Topaz, Rajka, Discovery (early), Rosette (red-fleshed), Katja (early), Beauty of Bath, Rubinette, Red Boskoop (cooker), Bramley (cooker) and Egremont Russet. There are also some delicious Irish apples available from the Irish Seed Savers Association.

These include, Sheep's Nose, Ard Cairn Russet, Bloody Butcher and many more.

For a self-sufficient large garden, I suggest to grow a mixture of about 12 apple trees with numerous varieties on different rootstocks. While an M9 rootstock grows quickly and you will get apples a couple of years after planting, you may need to wait up to 7 years for the very large growing trees on bigger rootstocks. If you plant M9, M26 and MM106 rootstocks at the same time, they will start to produce apples in different years. If you plan to grow a large orchard with MM106 rootstocks at a spacing of 10m apart, you could intercrop the gap with an M9 rootstock that will produce early and can stay for the first 10-15 years until the larger trees need the space.

If you have a medium-sized garden, my favourite rootstock is the M26. The trees grow to about 4m tall and I would space them about 5m apart. M26 has a much stronger root system compared to the M9 and will only need staking for 1 year, if grown in a sheltered garden.

Pruning

Correct pruning of apple trees is not easy and I think it is better not to prune than to prune badly.

A few guidelines:
- Use good secateurs (e.g. Felco).
- Don't over-prune - the more you cut off, the more upright growth you'll get.
- Prune out the 3 D's - dead, diseased and damaged wood.
- Prune out inward growing branches.
- Prune out rubbing branches.
- Prune new growth by half.
- Prune to an outward-facing bud.

Feeding apple trees

Over-feeding is nearly as bad as under-feeding. Sometimes an apple tree can be so vigorous and growing so well but never produces any fruit. The reason for that is there are too many nutrients (especially nitrogen) in the soil. If that's the case, stop feeding immediately and let grass grow around the base of the tree to compete with the trees for nutrients. My simple guideline is that if the annual growth is longer than 25cm, stop feeding. If the annual growth is only 15cm or less, you need to start feeding the tree.

It is best to cover the grass around the base of the apple tree under the crown with overlapping cardboard and cover the cardboard with 10cm composted manure or garden compost.
You may need to top it up if weeds push through.

Other Tree Fruit

While apples are the most reliable tree fruit for our climate, you can certainly grow a few others as well. Pears only do well in sunny and well-sheltered gardens, ideally trained as an espalier against a south-facing or south-east facing wall.
Plums, damsons and gages can be grown in an orchard, but for some reason, I only get a good yield every 3 to 4 years. Plums flower earlier and are often decimated by late frosts or spring gales. Cherries are my favourite fruits, but after many trials throughout the country, I gave up. Even if you manage to get an occasional crop, the birds will get them before you do.

Soft Fruit

No garden is complete without a soft fruit patch. Unfortunately, birds are just as keen on them as you are. You may need a bird netting or even a bird cage to protect them.

I suggest the following varieties:

Strawberries
Christina (early), Elsanta (mid) and Symphony (late)
Raspberries
Tulameen (summer fruiting), Autumn Bliss and All Gold (both autumn fruiting)
Gooseberries
Hinnonmaki Yellow, Hinnonmaki Red – these are incredibly tasty and reliable
Blackcurrants
Ben Sarek (early) and Ben Tirran (late)
Whitecurrants
White Pearl
Redcurrants
Junifer (early) and Rovada (late)
Rhubarb
Victoria
Blueberries
Blue Crop, Berkeley (please note that blueberries need special acidic soil)

Just one quick note about pruning soft fruit - while it's beyond the scope of this book to get into this in detail, there is one fruit that nearly always gets badly pruned – the blackcurrant.

Pruning blackcurrants
Never prune anything on the top of the plant but simply cut about one quarter of all the branches as close to ground level as possible. If there are 8 branches coming up from the base, you need to prune 2 or 3 branches at ground level. Pick the oldest, darkest ones. Blackcurrants fruit on last year's growth. So, if you cut at the top, you'll cut away next year's fruit.

Tea herbs

Most herbs are perennials and will last for many years. Only a few of the common herbs are annuals that need to be sown every year (parsley, summer savoury) or even every month (dill, coriander and chervil).

Annual herbs can be included in your vegetable rotation, but the perennial herbs will need to be grown in a separate bed, ideally a raised bed close to your kitchen.

Grow your own herbal tea

In a 2m² raised bed, you can grow a special mix of herbs which will give you the most delicious herbal tea fresh from your garden and an endless supply. There is no need to buy herbal tea bags any longer.

Collect a handful of a mixture of the herbs listed below, squeeze them in your hands to release the essential oils, place in a tea pot and pour boiling water into the pot and let it brew for 3-5 minutes.

Tea herb mixture:

Moroccan mint (grown separately in a large pot)
Lemon Thyme
Lemon Balm
Marjoram
Fennel (Bronze or Green)
Sage
Lemon Verbena

This is a basic recipe and you can add other herbs according to your taste. Enjoy!

Growing and selling vegetables

In your self-sufficient garden, you will always get gluts of certain vegetables, no matter how well you have planned your garden. A natural first step is to give the surplus away to friends and extended family.

Some people may feel that they would like to take it even more seriously and start a small market garden, selling vegetables, salads and herbs. Wouldn't it be great to turn hobby into a profession?

So many young people are now giving up their office jobs and becoming organic market gardeners. I have also come across people going into early retirement and finally doing what they always wanted to do.

Growing vegetables to make a living is not easy and requires a lot of experience, training and advice, as well as business skills.

It is, however, possible to make a good living and many Irish growers have shown that it is possible.

A more relaxed way is to simply grow a lot more food than you need and to sell it a various outlets.

You could have a small farm-gate shop at the entrance of your garden where customers leave money in an honesty box. Generally people are very honest.

Another option would be a local box scheme. You make up a number of vegetable boxes every week and put in whatever you have available. It requires some planning and people are often quite fussy.

Most health food shops, green-grocers and some larger shops (e.g. Supervalu) are keen to get local produce.

If you don't want to get into the money exchange, try bartering – you'll be surprised by what you may get back.

Blue Zones

Scientists have identified a number of so-called "Blue Zones" around the world where people live healthily into a very old age. The common denominators in all these zones is that people eat a wide diversity of vegetables and fruit, lead an active lifestyle even into old age (working in a garden) and having a solid social community.

Working in a garden, eating home-grown food, breathing fresh air, drinking unprocessed spring water and doing all this in company with friends and family - is this the secret to a healthy life? It nearly seems too easy but often the simplest things in life are the best!

If you are looking for a great retirement present for someone – buy them a polytunnel or a greenhouse.

Gardening Notes

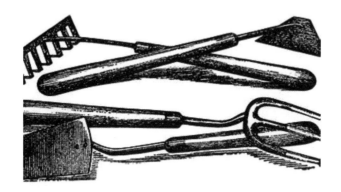

Planning

Crop Rotation

Seeds

Sowing

Planting

Harvesting

Storing

Thoughts of the day